METAPHYSICS

CASCADE COMPANIONS

The Christian theological tradition provides an embarrassment of riches: from scripture to modern scholarship, we are blessed with a vast and complex theological inheritance. And yet this feast of traditional riches is too frequently inaccessible to the general reader.

The Cascade Companions series addresses the challenge by publishing books that combine academic rigor with broad appeal and readability. They aim to introduce nonspecialist readers to that vital storehouse of authors, documents, themes, histories, arguments, and movements that comprise this heritage with brief yet compelling volumes.

TITLES IN THIS SERIES:

Phenomenology: A Basic Introduction in the Light of Jesus Christ by Donald Wallenfang
A Companion to the Mercersburg Theology by William B. Evans
Martin Luther as He Lived and Breated by Robert Kolb
Inhabiting the Land: Thiking Theologically about the Israeli-Palestinian Conflict by Alain Epp Weaver
Queer Theology by Linn Marie Tonstad
Understanding Pannenberg by Anthony C. Thiselton
The End is Music: A Companion to Robert W. Jenson's Theology by Chris E. W. Green
John Wesley: Optimist of Gracey by Henry H. Knight III
Called to Attraction: An Introduction to the Theology of Beauty by Brendan Thomas Sammon
A Primer in Ecotheology: Theology for a Fragile Earth by Celia E. Deane-Drummond
Postmodern Theology: A Biopic by Carl Raschke
The Becoming of God: Process Theology, Philosophy, and Multireligious Engagement by Roland Faber
Mimetic Theory and Biblical Interpretation: Reclaiming the Good News of the Gospel by Michael Hardin

METAPHYSICS

A Basic Introduction in a Christian Key

DONALD WALLENFANG

 CASCADE *Books* · Eugene, Oregon

METAPHYSICS
A Basic Introduction in a Christian Key

Cascade Companions

Copyright © 2019 Donald Wallenfang. All rights reserved. Except for brief quotations in critical publications or reviews, no part of this book may be reproduced in any manner without prior written permission from the publisher. Write: Permissions, Wipf and Stock Publishers, 199 W. 8th Ave., Suite 3, Eugene, OR 97401.

Cascade Books
An Imprint of Wipf and Stock Publishers
199 W. 8th Ave., Suite 3
Eugene, OR 97401

www.wipfandstock.com

PAPERBACK ISBN: 978-1-5326-4350-7
HARDCOVER ISBN: 978-1-5326-4351-4
EBOOK ISBN: 978-1-5326-4352-1

Cataloguing-in-Publication data:

Names: Wallenfang, Donald, author.
Title: Metaphysics : a basic introduction in a Christian key. / Donald Wallenfang.
Description: Eugene, OR : Cascade Books, 2019. | Series: Cascade Companions. | Includes index.
Identifiers: ISBN 978-1-5326-4350-7 (paperback) | ISBN 978-1-5326-4351-4 (hardcover) | ISBN 978-1-5326-4352-1 (ebook)
Subjects: LCSH: Metaphysics. | Theology. | Philosophical theology.
Classification: BD111 .W25 2019 (print) | BD111 .W25 (ebook)

Manufactured in the U.S.A.   SEPTEMBER 12, 2019

*To Saints Thomas Aquinas, Teresa Benedicta
of the Cross, and John Paul II*

"One might say that the saints are, so to speak,
new Christian constellations, in which the richness
of God's goodness is reflected. Their light, coming
from God, enables us to know better the interior
richness of God's great light, which we cannot
comprehend in the refulgence of its glory."

—Joseph Ratzinger, *Spirit of the Liturgy*, 111

TABLE OF CONTENTS

Introduction xi

CHAPTER 1: BEING 1

I. Being Itself (*ipsum esse*) and Beings (*entia*) 3
    A. Ontological Difference 3
    B. Unity and Diversity 4
    C. The Universal and the Particular 4
    D. First Contemplation 5

II. Form and Matter 7
    A. Hylomorphism 7
    B. Spiritual Being 9
    C. Contemplating Spirit 10
        1. Genealogy of Spirit 10
        2. Theological Turn 11
        3. Objective and Subjective Spirit 14
        4. Verbal Agency of Subjective Spirit 17

III. Substance 22
    A. Substance and Accidents 22
    B. Substance in the Concrete 23
    C. Substance in the Abstract 25

TABLE OF CONTENTS

    D. Essence and Existence 27

    E. Christology 29

IV. I Am 32

CHAPTER 2: FIRST PRINCIPLES 37

I. First Principles of Being 39

    A. The Good 39

    B. That Than Which Nothing Greater Can Be Thought 42

II. Laws of Logic 44

    A. The Principle of Non-contradiction 45

    B. The Principle of the Excluded Middle 47

    C. The Principle of Identity and Difference 49

III. "In the Beginning Was the *Logos*" (John 1:1) 50

CHAPTER 3: CAUSALITY 57

I. Act and Potency 60

II. Aristotle's Four Causes 67

    A. Material Cause 68

    B. Efficient Cause 68

    C. Formal Cause 70

    D. Final Cause 74

    E. Thomas Aquinas's Five Ways to Verify Divinity 77

        1. Act and Potency 78

        2. Efficient Cause and Effect 79

        3. Possibility and Necessity 79

        4. Gradations of Being 81

TABLE OF CONTENTS

    5. Intelligence and Final Cause 82
    6. I Am Received Being 83

III. "Whoever Believes in the Son Has Eternal Life" (John 3:36a) 85

CHAPTER 4: COSMOLOGY 90

I. Law and Order 94

II. Hierarchy of Being 95

III. The Transcendentals 101

IV. Eschatology 102

V. "The Redeemer of Man, Jesus Christ, Is the Center of the Universe and of History" (John Paul II, *Redemptor hominis*, 1) 104

CHAPTER 5: MORALITY 109

I. Do Good and Avoid Evil 111

II. Moral Law 116
    A. Eternal Law 118
    B. Natural Law 119
    C. Human/Civil Law 120
    D. Divine Law 121

III. Conscience 122

IV. A More Excellent Way 122

V. Morality Incomplete 125

Index 131

INTRODUCTION

For it is not lacking; if it were, it would lack everything.
 —*Parmenides* 8.33

A GRAND FAÇADE SPREADS across popular culture in every corner of the world. It can be described by many names: secularism, consumerism, materialism, shallow-mindedness, hedonism, pragmatism, superficiality. This façade is a worldview—a *Weltanschauung*—that fails to penetrate beneath the surface of things. It interprets the whole of reality in terms that can be reduced to the lowest common denominators of experience: casual laughter, cheap entertainment, fleeting thrills, pandering pleasures, ephemeral enjoyments (*jouissance, Genuß*). Within a postindustrial world there remains no time to contemplate. Asking why takes too long and involves too much energy that could be spent on gathering up more titillating stimuli that at least grant amnesty before the weight of being and the indictment of a guilty conscience. We have forgotten that we have forgotten.

In the wake of the Scientific Revolution and the Western Enlightenment, we have come to understand ourselves as matter in motion and rational agents who have the power to manipulate matter to conform it to our autobiographical standards of value. Instead of asking what is, we wonder what could be. Instead of concerning ourselves with the perennial question of being, we obsess over the terrestrial question of feeling. And feelings, too, we reduce to an interplay of chemicals within our bodies, rather than intuiting anything of spirit as distinct from matter. We have become enslaved to our self-made promises of progress. With our advanced technocratic powers, we have demolished the cultural edifices of our ancestors in favor of short-term gains and long-term losses. We have ravaged our forests and fields, and our souls, too, are left barren. We are in need of an elixir to lead us beyond the faithless façade of the pixels of pseudo-life. We are in need of a passion beyond passion that the decadent world neither knows nor recognizes, and that delivers a joy that cannot be taken away (see John 16:22). We are in need of a method—a *meta-hodós*—a way (*hodós*) beyond and behind (*meta*) the façade to grant access to the substance of being once again. And it is no coincidence that this new method is one of the oldest ones around: metaphysics.

There is physics and there is metaphysics. Physics, from the Greek word *phýsei*, meaning "nature," studies all that occurs in the natural order of being—that which we can observe with our bodily senses, measure, manipulate, and monitor. Physics seeks to understand the intrinsic laws of nature, from the tiniest theoretical particle to the most expansive reaches of astrophysics and space exploration. Physics happily manages the intelligible categories of matter, motion, and metrics. It informs its sister fields of chemistry, biology, and technology—all those investigative enterprises that comprise the natural sciences. Physics rules the day as the queen of all sciences in a world where time is money and matter is all that matters.

INTRODUCTION

However, for all its merits, physics gives intellectual entry to only part of the whole. Physics takes for granted the existence of its objects of study: the matrices of mass/energy amidst a spacetime continuum. Yet physics blushes before the following questions because it falls outside of its purview to ask them: Why is there something rather than nothing? What is being? What is the origin of the universe? Is there anything to reality besides mass/energy? Are there other types of causes besides material and efficient ones? If effects follow their anterior causes, what is the cause for which the universe is the effect? What are the essential elements of human being, and can these be reduced to mass/energy? Is there God? What are the attributes of divinity, and is it reasonable that God would communicate Godself to personal beings? What makes a person a person? These kinds of questions elude the scope and competencies of physics because they take us beyond the physical order of being alone. These questions are the foundation of two other specific fields of investigation that transgress the superficial boundaries of the natural sciences—two fields known historically as the original queen of all sciences and her handmaiden: theology and metaphysics.

At the start of the medieval university in the eleventh through thirteenth centuries in places like Bologna, Paris, Oxford, and Palencia, students were admitted to study theology only after mastering the other preliminary subjects of the liberal arts curriculum: grammar, logic, rhetoric, astronomy, geometry, arithmetic, music, and philosophy. Philosophy was defined by the categories of metaphysics, and these ultimately led to questions that were properly theological. While physics inquires about the external nature of beings, metaphysics (*meta* "beyond/behind" *phýsei* "nature") inquires about the internal nature of beings and being itself. Metaphysics is the science of being and beings. It considers being in its totality, even if this totality ultimately defies adequate comprehension. Metaphysics is a universal science because it is a science of universals. A term coined with reference to Aristotle's work entitled *ta meta ta physika* ("the [work] after the physics"), metaphysics probes much deeper into reality than the tools, resources, and questions of physics would allow. In a deductive direction, metaphysics begins first with principles of reason and being in order to understand what is real in a comprehensive way. Metaphysics recognizes that conclusions follow from their premises. Secondary truths follow primary truths.

For example, if we begin with the rational premise that a whole is greater than any one of its parts, we can conclude that a part is less than the whole of which it is only a part. To say that the part is greater than the whole, or that the whole is equal to the part, or that the whole is less than the part, is irrational. A second example: if we begin with the rational premise that a cause precedes its effect, we can conclude that an effect follows its prior cause. To say that an effect precedes its cause, or that a cause and its effect occur simultaneously, or that a cause follows its effect, is irrational. A more concrete example can be taken from the world of biology. Sunlight initiates the process of photosynthesis and not vice versa. Sunlight causes the process of photosynthesis to happen, and the process of photosynthesis does not cause the sun to emit photons. By adhering to logical deduction, metaphysics detects what must be the case about being and beings on the whole, ascending to intelligent encounter with universal truths in relation to particular cultural expressions of these truths.

Yet more than recounting the self-evident first principles and truths of metaphysics, this book wishes to guide the reader toward the invaluable benefits of thinking metaphysically. Above all, metaphysics will be presented as the

INTRODUCTION

gateway to contemplation and the foundation of sound ethical practice. Eleventh-century Muslim polymath Avicenna claimed that metaphysics was medicine for the spirit. What has inspired the writing of this book most is the fact of its present absence. Because this book did not exist, it had to be written. I could not find a book in English that presents the basics of metaphysics in a succinct, clear, manageable, and nonspecialized way. This book hopes to do just that. It inevitably will offend the sensibilities of specialists in metaphysics because of its broad generalizations and sweeping treatment of the historical evolution of metaphysics.

It must be admitted that there are many brands of metaphysics that have evolved to the present—for example, the classic metaphysics of Aristotle, René Descartes's metaphysics of subjectivity, and Emmanuel Levinas's ethical metaphysics. This book will concentrate on the classic metaphysics of Aristotle that was renewed and applied within the context of Christian theology by Thomas Aquinas in the thirteenth century. Aristotle was a master at asking the question "Why?" In fact, he dedicated an entire philosophical work toward it, entitled *Problems.* In this work, Aristotle asks "Why?" over nine hundred times! He considers subjects as diverse as medicine, mathematics, music, virtue, and the human body. Metaphysics is guided by the question of why in order to know what is true, good, and beautiful. Without pretending to provide an exhaustive systematic account of classic metaphysics, this book nevertheless will introduce the reader to the basic concepts, grammar, and logic of its method for investigating the real.

Greek philosophy—and all good philosophy for that matter—pursues truth with passion. As its name suggests, philosophy (from *philía*, "love" [of], and *sophía*, "wisdom") thirsts for encounter with truth, goodness, and beauty. Plato indicated that these three prizes are transcendent in

INTRODUCTION

nature. They lift us above what is most obvious in order to know what is most essential. When we make contact with the most essential forms of being, we call it good, beautiful, and true. Meanings matter much more than matter. And what do we find most meaningful, if not the most essential within our experience: things like joy, friendship, responsibility, hope, and love? Truth, goodness, and beauty indicate relationship. These transcendent experiences take place between the self and another not identical to the self. Moreover, we yearn to share such experiences with others in order that they would become even more fruitful (*paideía*) than our private enjoyment of them. And so we are brought again to the purpose of this book: to share the abundant fruits of thinking metaphysically.

Because I am a theologian (and not strictly a philosopher), I am concerned especially with tracing the fruitfulness of metaphysical thought within the domain of theology and, in my case, Christian theology. Metaphysics has played a tremendous role in theological development over the past two millennia of Christian belief and practice. It has ascended to the throne as the premier philosophical method within Christian thought. From the prevalence of Platonic (and Neoplatonic) philosophy within the early church to the renaissance of Aristotelian philosophy in the medieval universities, classic metaphysics has dominated within the Christian theological tradition, and with good reason. Metaphysics is the bedrock of perennial philosophy—those concepts and patterns of thought that are essentially timeless because they are essential and not transitory. Since metaphysics hits upon the immutable essences of things, there is much of its method that remains immutable. For example, Plato was very enamored of geometry. In fact, an inscription was posted above the main entrance to his academy that read "Let no man ignorant of

INTRODUCTION

geometry enter." Geometric shapes such as circles, squares, triangles, and rectangles, as well as lines, vectors, and arcs, reveal something of eternity. As pure abstract forms, they are indelible, and their geometric formulas are the same yesterday, today, and forever. The circle always has been and always will be the same form. For Plato, forms and ideas (as abstracted from matter) are that which is most real.

Plato's most notable disciple, Aristotle, extended Plato's predilection for form and augmented it with a more complete description of the integral relationship between form and matter. Aristotle's philosophical worldview is known to this day as hylomorphism, derived from the Greek words for matter (*hýle*) and form (*morphé*). Without negating the primacy of form, Aristotle filled out Plato's understanding of the real by giving a bit more attention and value to matter. Christianity benefitted greatly from the Greek philosophical legacy as the religion took root around the Mediterranean Basin and spread geographically from there. Metaphysics provided a philosophical foundation upon which the rational and realist theology of Christianity was able to find stable and lasting footing. Christianity is so intertwined with metaphysics that any attempt to do Christian theology without metaphysics invalidates the theological project to the degree that it is no longer recognizable as authentically Christian. It is not that Jesus, the itinerant Jewish rabbi, can be placed historically or culturally in the line of Greek philosophers. After all, the teaching of Jesus consists not so much of systematic philosophical reasoning as it does of a witness to divine revelation in word and deed. Nevertheless, we do perceive a common genus that encompasses Athens and Jerusalem: truth cannot contradict truth. Reason and revelation integrated gives us the full picture of truth.

INTRODUCTION

In order to let the fertile intertwining of reason and divine revelation take place, this book will portray Jesus as metaphysician par excellence. Just as Justin the Martyr testified: the *logos* of reason is the *Logos* of faith. Jesus is presented as the great physician in the Gospels. He is witnessed healing many people of physical and psychological infirmities. He restores sense and movement. He exorcises demons. He gives *ex nihilo* nourishment to famished people. He resuscitates the dead back to life. Yet all of these miraculous—indeed supernatural—works are intended to point to something else: the advent of the kingdom of God. They are a foretaste of the fullness of life to come beyond (*meta*) the grave because there is something—better someone—that/who is behind (*meta*) nature (*phýsei*) all along: divine Being (as verb more so than as noun); that is, at the same time, the Reason (*Logos*) for all beings. In this way, because Jesus is at once the fullness of humanity and divinity, he is not only the great physician, but the great metaphysician as well. For instance, through his parabolic teachings, Jesus leads us to that which is beyond (*meta*) the surface of life, from seeds, money, and clothing to what is even more essential: the kingdom of God and its witnesses woven together with the threads of divine love tugged along by the precious piercing needle that penetrates flesh and wood.

Once again, this book will attempt to keep its presentation of metaphysics and its application within Christian theology as simple as possible. The book is written for a general audience of nonexperts. Definitions and explanations of concepts will be kept brief for the sake of clarity and readability. Every chapter will be organized according to the most primary concepts of metaphysics. Also, each chapter will feature candid examples of how metaphysical thinking can be incorporated into daily life, as well as interaction with Scripture as it pertains to metaphysics. I write

INTRODUCTION

in the English language, bearing in mind that metaphysics did not originate or evolve significantly in an English-speaking world. Aristotle wrote in Greek, Thomas Aquinas wrote in Latin, and Edith Stein wrote in German. Nevertheless, I write with the confidence that truth is translatable and destined to be inculturated into the myriad of cultures around the world, my own included. In the highest place, the truth of the Gospel of Jesus, along with its handmaiden of metaphysics, comes to its full form to the extent that it is inculturated according to a unified harmony of expression. My intent is not to suggest that encounter with Jesus leads us to the ultimate end of encounter with metaphysics, but rather the other way around: I will argue that greater familiarity with metaphysics brings about greater familiarity with Jesus of Nazareth. Metaphysics predisposes us for more intimate and meaningful encounter with Jesus. For those readers wishing to delve deeper into theological metaphysics, I recommend to you my previous book, *Human and Divine Being: A Study on the Theological Anthropology of Edith Stein*. The present book may serve as a helpful primer and/or companion to *Human and Divine Being*.

Let the reader be assured that I am not unfamiliar with German philosopher Friedrich Nietzsche's decisive critiques that deconstruct the pretentiousness of metaphysics and proclaim the death of God, namely, the God of metaphysics, and the twilight of nihilism. Nor am I unaware of French philosopher Jacques Derrida's persuasive accusation of the tautological character of metaphysics as sheer *différance*, that is, the difference and deferral of meaning within the nomenclature of metaphysics that incessantly passes the buck of meaning to the degree that there are no truly static and stable meanings in its superlative assertions. In fact I regard these philosophical projects as quite helpful for resuscitating what is most essential in metaphysics

INTRODUCTION

and leaving behind its drosses of covert and, at times, ostentatious prestige, privilege, and power. If there be any real and profitable metaphysics, it will be a humble metaphysics—indeed, a humiliated metaphysics. My aspiration behind (*meta*) this book is to humiliate the humiliation of metaphysics in order for it to regain its indispensable role for seeking truth in every nook and cranny where it can be found—including, and above all, that architecture behind (*meta*) the edifice of creation in which all nooks and crannies emerge, always in relation to being.

Donald Lee Wallenfang, OCDS/
Emmanuel Mary of the Cross
Memorial of Saint John Paul II
October 22, 2018

1

BEING

To be, or not to be: that is the question.
—Shakespeare, *Hamlet*, 3.1

הָיָה. εἰμί. τὸ ὄν. οὐσία. *Esse. Ens. Ser. Être. Essere. Sein. Wesen.* Being. What is being? This may be the most basic and yet most sophisticated question that we human beings can ask. It is the premier philosophical question across cultures and traditions since time immemorial. Aristotle considered this question to commence all subsequent philosophy. It was the question that initiated first philosophy, and all other questions relate back to it as to their most ancient ancestor. To ask the question of being (*die Seinsfrage*) is to ask everything all at once. The question of being encompasses everything because anything that is has being. Even the concept of nothingness has a kind of being (if only in the form of negation), always in relation to being. Being is first before subtracting anything from it. If there is less it is

METAPHYSICS

because first there was more. In the beginning, all. In the end, all. In the beginning, to be. In the end, to be. Being before beginning. Being after end. For being, beginning is end and end is beginning because being is is. Being prior to existence because anything that exists stands out (from *ex*, "out," and *sistere*, "to cause to stand") in its being thanks to being. Being before me because it is clear that there was a time—most of the time—when I was not. Thanks to being, I am.

Being itself (*ipsum esse*) cannot be measured. Numbers are because of being. Being itself is not an object. Objects are because of being. Being itself does not move from one place to another. Movement and places are because of being. Being itself cannot be found within the universe or be regarded as identical to the universe. The universe is because of being. Being itself does not change. Change is because of being. Being itself is being because being is the be-cause—the cause that is—the cause of itself (*causa sui*) and the cause of each and every being (*ens*) and, therefore, the cause of all beings (*entia*). What is being? Is. What is being? Be-cause. What is being? Yes. What is being? To be. What is being? All. What is being? The whole. What is being? Not nothing. What is being? Not lacking.

The question of being opens onto contemplation of all things (and non-things). It generates not so much a Pandora's box of complexities as an infinite treasure box of discoveries. The question of being is implied in every why question. Why? Be-cause. Whenever we ask why, we inquire into the cause of a perceived effect. Ultimately, we inquire into the cause that is the cause of all unnecessary and contingent causes. Why is the sky blue? Why is the earth round? Why does the sun shine? Why are there waves in the ocean? Why am I here? Why is there a universe? Why is there something rather than nothing? The fact that we ask these questions suggests the fact that their answers precede them. We would not ask such "why" questions if there was no rational "because" in response to them. This rational "because" is another name for truth. Metaphysics asks the question of being because it is asking the truth about being. It is this truth that this book yearns to contemplate and share with you, the reader.

I. BEING ITSELF (*IPSUM ESSE*) AND BEINGS (*ENTIA*)

A. Ontological Difference

A term that runs almost synonymously with metaphysics is ontology (from *ón*, "being," and *lógos*, "science"), the science of being. One key distinction sets the field for all other distinctions in metaphysics: the ontological difference between being itself (*ipsum esse*) and beings (*entia*). I use the Latin terms as employed by Thomas Aquinas to help differentiate between the two concepts. Being itself (*ipsum esse*) refers to being in a verbal sense of the word: the very act of being, or existence itself. Existence does not fluctuate between there and not there because it defines everywhere. Simply put, it is. This is the primary term and the necessary condition of possibility for all individual beings that have existence. The second term of the ontological difference, beings (*entia*), refers to everything that has being (or existence) but is not identical to being (or existence) in itself. We can say that all nominative beings (*entia*) share in the oneness of existence, however, existence itself (*ipsum esse*) is not a being per se. Rather, existence itself (*ipsum esse*) encompasses and transcends all beings (*entia*) while giving them a share in being. So the first distinction for metaphysics is that between being itself (*ipsum esse*) on the one hand,

and beings (*entia*) on the other. Without this vital distinction, I may end up thinking that I am at the center of the universe after all. Instead, in truth, I recognize that I am a being among beings that share in a common existence, and that no individual being welcomed itself into existence. Being itself grants being to all contingent individual beings not identical to being itself. From where else would they have been adopted into being? So far we have determined what all beings have in common, namely, being (or existence), but also that beings themselves are differentiated from being itself (*ipsum esse*) and from one another according to their individuality.

B. Unity and Diversity

Following the ontological difference between being itself and beings, metaphysics points to a second key distinction: that between unity and diversity, or between singularity and plurality. All numbers are based upon the number one. The numbers two, three, and four, for instance, are multiples of one. How many existences are there? One. How many instances of being itself (*ipsum esse*) are there? One. To say otherwise would be nonsensical inasmuch as all concepts of being relate back to the fundamental concept of being itself (*ipsum esse*) that encompasses every episode and indication of being. Yet how many beings do I encounter in my experience? Innumerable. Just as there is a oneness of being, there is a multiplicity of beings. Being is one yet many. It is united yet diverse. It is singular yet plural.

C. The Universal and the Particular

The third distinction related to the primary distinction of the ontological difference is that between the universal and the particular. Closely related to the previous distinction between unity and diversity, the concept of universality encompasses and applies to all beings, whereas the concept of particularity signifies individual beings diversified one from the other. When we contemplate being, we draw these distinctions in order to know being in truth, in its variegated unity and universality. There is a wholeness of being, yet this wholeness is comprised of many parts, and these parts, too, are composed of many particles. It is not that there is empirical (from *empeiría*, "experience") natural science on the one hand and nonempirical metaphysics on the other. Rather, a common verifiability obtains for all thought in relation to truth. Particular experiences receive their standards of measurement and verifiability from the universality of truth. The self-evidence of particular existing individual beings is oriented according to the self-evidence of universal being itself (*ipsum esse*).

D. First Contemplation

The question of being sparks contemplation. This question has led many saints and mystics over the course of human history to ecstatic experiences and lives of heroic virtue. For example, Julian of Norwich recounts a vision she had of a small spherical object in the palm of her hand that she describes as no larger than a hazelnut. Upon contemplating the being of this tiny object, she was led to contemplation of the entire universe and to being itself. She was filled with the intuition that the being of this small thing never would go out of existence inasmuch as it was loved by God. She realized that everything had being and that its being would last as long as God loved it. And insofar as God is being itself (*ipsum esse*), God could do nothing other than love always and without ceasing what God has loved into being.

METAPHYSICS

Twentieth-century English mystic Caryll Houselander also describes the possibility of contemplating the entire universe according to the sensational pattern of a miniature snowflake. She calls the experience an inscape. An inscape is when the fullness and universality of being itself is revealed in a very small particular being that bears the imprint of the cosmos—a cosmos that is ordered according to the essential patterns of being, such as distinctive forms, symmetry and the provocation of beauty.

Figure 1

I know of a man who had a similar experience while eating shrimp mei fun for lunch in a Chinese restaurant. As the story goes, he was enjoying his meal in solitude and looked over at the neon sign in the front window of the restaurant. A miniscule piece of fuzz was dangling from the sign. Upon seeing the microscopic fiber suspended in midair, he was overwhelmed with a sense of gratitude over the goodness that it, too, has being. This infinitesimal being disclosed the infinity of being itself (*ipsum esse*) even by itself. This shows the creative and powerful potential of contemplation based on the question of being: it awakens deep thanksgiving upon recognizing that all being—including my own being—receives itself as a gift from an infinite elsewhere that is nonidentical to the caducity of mutable finite being.

II. FORM AND MATTER

A. Hylomorphism

Once deciphering the ontological difference between being itself (*ipsum esse*) and beings (*entia*), we can proceed to define being more precisely: matter (*hýle*) and form (*morphé*). As a philosophical worldview developed by Aristotle, hylomorphism refers to an integrated and holistic way of comprehending being according to its two primary components: matter and form. In the realm of being, we are most familiar with matter. Objects. Atoms. Stuff. The periodic table of elements. What I can buy at a store. Not only is matter most familiar to us because it is what we perceive most immediately with our senses, but matter is also what we can measure, manipulate, and manufacture. We can understand it to a high degree because it is what is outside of us, even including the material extension of our own bodies. However, metaphysics reminds us that matter always has some specific form. Without form, no actual matter. Pure theoretical matter is pure potency, yet pure potency without form is nonbeing insofar as it remains non-actualized being. Form is what actualizes matter into actual being. The tiniest subatomic particles, too, have form, and so they exist. What differentiates one type of subatomic particle from another, whether proton, electron, or quark? Form. What differentiates one element from another, whether hydrogen, oxygen or carbon? Form. What differentiates one kind of being from another, whether elephant, eagle or human? Form. This may seem like stating the obvious, but it is one of the crucial first principles of metaphysics: form precedes matter. This principle reflects the exact relationship between being itself and beings: being itself precedes beings.

Form signifies cause. Form is what effects matter and causes it to adhere to innumerable shapes and qualities of being. Because form acts on matter, a specific being becomes itself. For example, before a house can be built, a blueprint must be created by an architect. Architecture precedes construction. Ideas precede their material instantiation. The form of a circle precedes the making of a wheel. The form (genus) *Hippocampus* precedes the fifty-four species of seahorse, both on a microlevel (conception of a new individual organism and its ongoing development) and on a macrolevel (the process of biological evolution that developed toward the distinct genus and species of the organism known today as seahorse). There are organisms because they are organized according to specific forms of being. The target precedes the trajectory of the shot. If the shot has a goal, a target has been determined in advance. Matter adapts to the formal agency exercised upon it. Matter is organized according to the organs of form. Related to the Greek word for work (*érgon*), an organ is what serves to actualize a particular function of an organism in light of particular ends. Organic forms shape and structure matter so as to diversify being and promote the perpetuation of life. Though not reducible to matter, form is the immaterial pattern of being that must precede the material manifestation of a specific pattern of being. Just as feelings, ideas, and words precede speech, form precedes the respective patterns of matter that adhere in direct relation to predetermined ends of activity. Because cause precedes effect, form precedes matter. Every instance of matter is always already formed matter.

B. Spiritual Being

If pure matter (*materia prima*) is pure potency, then pure form is pure act. If matter is expressed externally as born-out composite form (made up of parts), then form is expressed internally as inhaled or animated noncomposite spirit (not made up of parts). Forms, as forms abstracted from matter, are spiritual objects. Without implying a specific religious tradition or divine revelation, a first-level (philosophical) reflection on the question of being proffers two distinct counterparts of being: spirit and matter. Concepts such as will, agency, freedom, person, love, and gift depend entirely on an immaterial region of being called spirit. Spirit is that which animates matter. Spirit is that which acts on matter to modify its structure and composition. Spirit is that which investigates matter from a zero point of personal orientation from the inside out. Spirit is not what is added on to matter as a superficial quasi-religious layer of externality upon externality. Rather, spirit is the recognition and certification of the interiority of being from an interior standpoint of being. Because we are composed of a spiritual dimension within our personal embodied being, we are able to detect this spiritual dimension within everything that has being. So we have arrived at a more precise description of being itself (*ipsum esse*): pure form, pure spirit—by definition, immaterial, inasmuch as form/spirit/act precedes matter/potency.

C. Contemplating Spirit

1. Genealogy of Spirit

It is difficult to describe that which is doing the describing. This refers precisely to the task of spirit trying to describe spirit. It is much easier to talk about matter (and its pieces) that does not describe what it is and is not identical to spirit. To this point, metaphysics has allowed us to put being itself, form and spirit, into semi-comprehension always in relation to matter. I say semi-comprehension because being itself, form and spirit, are posited as necessary conditions of possibility for matter and its plethora of organic forms, but spiritual being itself is that which does the informing. Being itself, form and spirit, cannot be seized upon as clear intelligible objects for thought because they are abstractions of abstraction. When I abstract the circle from the wheel of the wagon, I have abstracted once. But when I abstract the human soul from itself as the one abstracting the shape circle from the wagon wheel, I have abstracted twice and am left with no static material image of the soul in itself.

The soul is the form of the body (*anima forma corporis*) in the way interiority is related to exteriority. Spirit animates matter from the inside out in formal movements such as creation, generation, and unfolding. Spirit is the raison d'être—the reason for all being, including its own. Spirit spirates, or breathes form into matter, to give matter individuality, communal existence, and purpose. With no spiration of spirit, there would be no purposefulness of matter—no evolution or development of being. Even more, with no spirit, there would be no being to speak of because matter would be left unformed (including the formal concept of prime matter) and, therefore, nonexistent. Point out to me a piece of unformed matter and you will have overturned the foundation of metaphysics and everything I wish to say in this book.

Contemplating spiritual being opens perception to the ontological depth of creatures. No being has given itself being, but instead has received its being that can be described as radically contingent, dependent, unnecessary, mutable, ephemeral and finite—that is, limited. No finite being is being itself. Not even the incalculable sum total of finite beings is infinite altogether and by itself. This much is certain. With this realization comes the wonder and awe of receiving one's existence, not just once, but at every instant. In other words, my being is being granted to me at each moment. I begin to marvel more and more at my feeble being that depends on an ontological source totally other than me. I am overcome by the glory of being—being itself—that without question is the eternal forerunner of my received frail being and all that it might reflect of eternal uncreated being's nobility.

2. Theological Turn

Twentieth-century mystic and martyr Edith Stein contemplated spiritual being to a high degree. Her tomes in philosophy and theology, as well as her spiritual writings, letters, and autobiography, attest to a soul who was enraptured by spiritual being. She was convinced of the intersection between philosophy and theology and did not hesitate to identify eternal spiritual being with divinity. Yes, even philosophy can demonstrate the existence of God—being itself (*ipsum esse*), at least through the mode of analogy—with utmost rational certainty. Philosophy can ascertain that God exists, but it is not philosophy's purview to determine who this God is. The revelation of the divine Who belongs to God alone. It is left to God to speak Godself to personal spiritual creatures who yearn to know the eternal raison d'être—the *Logos* of all created and finite being, both spiritual and material.

Theology is the science of divine revelation (*sacra scientia/sacra doctrina*) that extends the scope of reason and knowledge further than philosophy can take it. It is one thing to have knowledge (*scientia/gnosis*); it is another thing to be known, especially to be known by God (*gnosthésomai*; see Gal 4:9). Theology reveals a knowledge deeper than facts, figures, and objects—even a knowledge more meaningful and relevant than all that metaphysics by itself could compile and systematize: "We realize that 'all of us have knowledge'; knowledge inflates with pride, but love builds up. If anyone supposes he knows something, he does not yet know as he ought to know. But if one loves God, one is known by him" (1 Cor 8:1b–3).[1] Through the intentionality of faith in God's self-revelation, theology gives access to a luminous clarity of the first principles of metaphysics that reason alone cannot intuit. Reason alone can know that God is and (to some measure) what God is, but reason alone cannot know who God is. The personal who-ness of God is for God alone to disclose. Only God speaks well of God.

---

1. Unless otherwise noted, all Scripture citations in this book come from the NABRE.

BEING

Figure 2

As a theologian, I can play the game of methodological atheism and theological indifference for only so long. I can masquerade as a self-sufficient philosopher only until the clock strikes midnight. There comes a point, usually quite early on, when I can delay no more to cast my cards on the table and claim the ace of spades: divinity. I have something to do with something because Something had something to do with me. I am someone because Someone is from eternity. There is something rather than nothing. Among this something there are someones rather than only somethings. Because there is something rather than nothing, and because I experience myself and others as someones, the eternal something that is—being itself—is eternal Someone(s). Eternity is personal inasmuch as I am a person. Being itself precedes beings. Form precedes matter. Act precedes potency. Cause precedes effect. Kenosis precedes kinesis. Spirit precedes matter. Eternal Spirit precedes finite created spirits. The infinite precedes the finite. Initiation of gift precedes receptivity to gift. Limitation is delimited by that which is unlimited because the limen between the infinite and the finite is *creatio ex nihilo*.

METAPHYSICS

And so marks the decisive moment of this book—the time has come for the cat to come out of the bag. Not *deus ex machina*, because *machina a Deo*. It is impossible not to refer to God when speaking about first principles and form and actuality and causality and being because God is the perfect Actuality that makes impossibility impossible. If it were not so, there would be nothing rather than something, which is certainly not the case. In calling upon the living witness of Edith Stein, we have secured the warrant for proceeding toward our intended end: theological metaphysics. Any metaphysics that does not dilate according to the systolic pulse of divine revelation succumbs to metaphysics in effigy; that is, half-baked rationality. So I will not hesitate to refer to divinity, God, Jesus, or the Trinity, since methodological atheism serves only to reinforce the caducity of being without Being itself (*ipsum esse subsistens omnibus modis indeterminatum*, "self-subsistent being unlimited in every way"). As I call upon Edith Stein, who insists on the rapprochement between philosophy and theology, to testify to truth by referring the reader to her own life and works, I, at the same time, wager my own testimony to truth by running directly to the source, Who was running directly towards me before the awakened time of creation.

3. Objective and Subjective Spirit

So may we tarry together a while longer to contemplate spiritual being now that an apology for explicit reference to divinity has been made. Metaphysics reveals spiritual being as the necessary condition of possibility for material being, for act precedes potency and form precedes matter. What are act and form if not spirit? What is being itself if not divine Spirit? Theological metaphysics personalizes what otherwise would be rather sterile and generic categories of being. Meant by the concept spirit is personal self-giving, interiority, proximity, love, call, response, and responsibility for the other. The God revealed in Jesus of Nazareth is the Most Holy Trinity—Father, Son, and Holy Spirit—a communion of divine persons that generates the cosmos as a way to share their eternal refulgence of being with that which did not exist along with God before eternity. Spirit gives being inasmuch as we who once had no being have received our being from a whence that did not ask our permission to exist. And yet we do exist. So we contemplate this divine Whence who ordained our being with respect to his own.

Being is dynamic, beginning with spiritual being. Spirit gives being. Spirit orders and orchestrates being. Spirit moves and forms being. It is no coincidence that cognate meanings of spirit are wind and breath (*ruach*; *pneuma*; *spiritus*), for wind signifies the power of motion and breath connotes life. There are two distinct kinds of spiritual being: objective spirit and subjective spirit. Objective spiritual beings are the impersonal forms that constitute the stable and definitive natures of all finite existents. Forms such as geometric shapes, numbers, meanings, distinct species of biological being (according to their inner psychological life, whether vegetative or sentient), and eidetic objects (for example, incorporeal ideas and concepts). Being is organized according to the differentiated forms it takes, each form in relation to others. All such forms originate in the mind of God and, because God thinks them, they exist. Overcoming the nominalist heresy of the ambiguity of names, objective spiritual beings manifest themselves by themselves with an ontological stability at once immutable and incommunicable. Universals do exist after all because being precedes naming.

METAPHYSICS

Subjective spiritual beings are persons. Within the order of creation, only two types of personal spiritual beings exist: angels (finite personal spiritual beings) and humans (finite personal spiritual and material beings). Divinity (infinite personal spiritual being), as Trinity, is also thought (because self-revealed) in terms of personhood, namely, God the Father, God the Son, and God the Holy Spirit. Subjective spiritual beings are those who deal with objective spiritual beings. We recognize objective spiritual beings because we abstract from matter and contemplate being. Even the concept of matter in itself is an objective spiritual being. There is no meaning that is not inherently spiritual.

In a negative sense, what we mean by spirit is that which cannot be reduced to matter alone as matter per se. If all were matter and only matter, it would not abstract from itself or turn and face itself as a genuine other because there would be no personal spiritual self to address it. In other words, if matter was all that existed, it would not matter to itself. Instead we experience the radical otherness of personal interiority in relation to impersonal exteriority. Matter matters because there is something (someone!) other than matter, otherwise matter would go unrecognized as such. No atom is a person. No element of the periodic table is a person. No molecule is a person. No biological species without the intrinsic (at least *in potentia* by nature) rational capacities of intellectuality, freedom and self-giving love is a person. No corpse is a person. Personhood implies subjective spiritual being that is living and active (at least *in potentia* or even disabled), as well as receptively passive to the active self-donation of other persons. Subjective spiritual beings (persons) are those who abstract from matter and intuit and intend objective spiritual beings. We abstract from the particular and know universals. Aristotle indicates that universals are the most difficult things for us to know because they are furthest from the senses.[2] Nevertheless, subjective spiritual being is able to know universals through the media of the senses, but also by necessarily abstracting from them through the agent intellect.

For example, history has taught us the importance of thinking human nature universally and inclusively. Genocide is the consequence of failing to think metaphysically. If certain persons are categorized systematically as nonpersons, they will not be treated as persons. Yet metaphysics delivers the truth of a universal human nature that encompasses the diversity of ethnic, racial, sexual, developmental, and economic (and every other) particularity. For metaphysics, the universality of human nature finds its basis in the evidence of the rational soul. This is what is intrinsically unique to human beings among all other material and biological existents. Without recourse to universal natures of being, especially that of our own, we are left to the arbitrary reductionisms to particularity, disastrous categorical mistakes, and the self-concerned will to power (Nietzsche). The truths and first principles of metaphysics prevent us from interpreting ourselves as less than we really are. They also keep us from interpreting other impersonal beings as more than they really are. We can personify imaginatively any impersonal being in the universe only to the degree that we ourselves are persons. Metaphysics inspires us to call a thing what it is in every aspect of its being.

4. Verbal Agency of Subjective Spirit

Subjective spiritual being signifies personal agency of action. The word being operates as a nominative verb in this sense. Subjective spiritual being refers to the person (noun) who persons (verb); it refers to the personal spirit (noun)

2. Aristotle, *Metaph* 1.2.

who spirits (verb)—the personal spiritual being who respires (breathes), inspires (motivates), perspires (works), aspires (intellectualizes), conspires (collaborates), and expires (gives to the point of abandonment) in relation to other beings. In classic terms, subjective spiritual being implies a personal will to act. Not as some nebulous dark matter that can be situated within the mass/energy network of physics, subjective spiritual being is what generates being by infusing it with form (from the standpoint of divinity), and what intellectually (vis-à-vis truth), affectively (vis-à-vis beauty) and morally (vis-à-vis goodness) receives these infused forms with delight (from the standpoint of humanity and angelity). Writing a book itself is an exercise of subjective spiritual being. Thoughts come to mind, and I desire to communicate these with other persons. Reading a book, too, is an exercise of subjective spiritual being. Meanings (spiritual objects) leap off the page from text to conscious recognition. Meaning unfurls meaning like a Sefer Torah that unrolls with infinite twists and turns. Subjective spiritual being is the very causality of meaning. We receive and generate meaning to the degree that we cannot be reduced (reduce ourselves!) to meaninglessness. Nihilism, too, has meaning, and so does everything under the sun for us subjective spiritual beings.

Figure 3

I am. Personalized being. I am. You are. S/he is. They are. We are. Personal pronouns signify the veracity of subjective spiritual being. Call me an "it" and you have failed to recognize the truth of my metaphysical being. Subjective spiritual being is being personalized because someone (and not only something) has come on the scene of being. The typical problem we have with metaphysics is that we want to convert every aspect of being into material objects that have surface to be sensed exteriorly. However, the superficial surface of being only really serves to testify to its core: spirit. Exteriority obtains to the measure that it proceeds out (*ex*) from its native ground (*terra*), namely, spiritual interiority. At the center of matter is not matter, but spirit. To say spirit is to reach the irreducible interiority of being—that zero point of orientation of every fragment of being—and, at the same time, to witness to that subzero point of orientation of being itself, the living Interiority from which every interiority is named. Or to personalize this intuition better:

METAPHYSICS

> For this reason I kneel before the Father [*patér*], from whom every family [*patriá*] in heaven and on earth is named, that he may grant you in accord with the riches of his glory to be strengthened with power through his Spirit in the inner self, and that Christ may dwell in your hearts through faith; that you, rooted and grounded in love, may have strength to comprehend with all the holy ones what is the breadth and length and height and depth, and to know the love of Christ that surpasses knowledge, so that you may be filled with all the fullness of God. (Eph 3:14–19)

God the Father, creator of the heavens and the earth, is the Form of forms, the Act of acts, the Cause of causes, the Being of beings, and the Interiority of interiority. Teresa of Avila maintains that the human soul is an interior castle in which God finds a home. The fertile metaphor of divine fatherhood escorts us to encounter with a God who desires to dwell on the inside of created being because God dwells on the inside of God from eternity. If there is an outside, there is an inside, and it is because of this inside that there is an outside. We dissect being from the outside in because we want to know it from the inside out. Spirit is what can be dissected no further into parts. It is the fundamental formal substratum of every being. Why not dissect being thoroughly instead of being content to dissect only the epithelial layers and mistake these residual parts for the whole? Metaphysics goes further than skin-deep, and further than bone marrow, cellular nuclei, axons and dendrites, nucleic acids, and cardiac chambers of the body. Metaphysics carries out its dissection of being all the way to its personal spiritual impetus that seeks, rushes towards, and attacks (*impetere*) only to attach, claim, and share. Through metaphysics, we gradually discover a cosmic epiphany of being self-revealed

BEING

from interior to exterior, yet discernable from exterior to interior.

Paul's words from prison to the church in Ephesus attest to the veracity and expansiveness of the inner self that no physical barriers, chains, or locks could detain. Spiritual being is not contingent on spatial coordinates because all space is coordinated by it. Spiritual being is not measurable by chronological time because it creates time according to its own kairological prerogatives. Spiritual being is not confined to the determined course of atoms and their constituent particles because it determines them according to its own appanages of love. Subjective spiritual being, as radical interiority, yearns to know the breadth and length and height and depth of being, yet experiences this very knowledge as a paradoxical inversion of apodictic knowledge. To be acquainted with the fullness of being is to have the acquaintance of Jesus—a friendship that surpasses knowledge (*gnosis*) as mental objects to index with the mind. More precisely, to know Jesus is to be known by Jesus and to be filled with all the fullness of God rather than to possess it as object or private property. Subjective spiritual being is the personal capacity to receive the fullness of divine being that, though not composed of matter from beyond eternity, creates matter from nothing, making it something, and unites himself to finite matter and spirit (incarnation) in order to transfigure its forlorn drift of entropy into a metamorphosis of glory.

As personal interiority in relation to exteriority, subjective spiritual being is incorporeal in its essence—simple, not composed of parts, yet individuated, each angel or soul distinct from the other. Indestructible and rationally conscious individuality-in-relation is the essence of subjective spiritual being. Subjective spiritual being is inherently relational because relationship—personal relationship in particular—is the vital medium of self-communication, self-donation, and receptivity and responsibility for the other as gift. Personal relationship is the medium of love. Though such meanings begin to pull away from the grammar, logic, and rhetoric of metaphysics (because they are properly phenomenological), they are fitting to cite here, at least to hint at a more comprehensive description of subjective spiritual being that must be augmented by phenomenology. For the purposes of this book, however, we will confine ourselves to a strict metaphysical analysis of being rather than lean too far into the territory of phenomenology. To this end, we will continue our initial attempt to lay a foundation for metaphysics by considering another concept indispensable for understanding being: substance.

III. SUBSTANCE

A. Substance and Accidents

In Book Seven of his *Metaphysics*, Aristotle crystallizes the premier question of first philosophy. He says that to ask "What is being?" is to ask "What is substance (*ousía*)?" Aristotle rephrases the question of being in this way because metaphysics aims at discovering the first principles of being—those irreducible substrates upon which all beings rest as themselves and as distinct from one another. The question of being aims at the core of being. What is at the heart of being? This question does not confine itself to anatomy, physiology, and physics alone, but, again, pursues the intrinsic and peculiar natures of things. Aristotle draws the distinction between substance and the accidental properties (accidents) of a given substance. Substance is what a being is—for example, human, horse, water, angel, or mushroom. Substance is the universal that applies to all beings of a given genus or species. Accident is what is incidental, nonessential, or particular to a universal substance—for example, large, small, brown, hot, healthy, ill, hard, soft, long, short, abled, disabled, rich, poor, weak, strong, etc. In addition, a metaphysics of substance implies a metaphysics of presence. Substances are present (from *prae*, "to be before one, at hand," and *esse*, "being") to the mind because they are in proximity to perception and present themselves to be known in conscious rational thought. All substances discussed in metaphysics are rooted in sense perceptions of different beings and abstraction from these concrete perceptions. Because beings are present before the metaphysician, s/he is able to contemplate their specific substances. So what more can be said about substance?

B. Substance in the Concrete

Instead of continuing with an abstract definition of an abstract concept, let us begin with a very important concrete question: What is the human being? Is this question not at the same time asking another question: What is the human person? In the early sixth century, Roman philosopher Boethius, in his letter to John the Deacon concerning the metaphysical personal identity of Jesus, defined him in this way: *naturae rationalis individua substantia* ("an individual substance of a rational nature"). The term substance is integral to the Boethian definition of person. What kind of being is a person? A rock? A tree? A star? An insect? An ape? A bacterium? None of these, because they all lack a distinctive rational nature. A human being? Yes, because humans are rational agents of being, exhibiting ample evidence of rationality, namely, culture, yet more precisely intellectuality, freedom, and the capacity to love and to be loved (even *in potentia*) as persons by other persons. Without an adequate universal definition of personhood as applied to human

METAPHYSICS

beings, how could we point to a common human nature? Without such a definition, we would be left to the whims of the arbitrary will to power of the powerful and the slough of dehumanizing -isms (all based on some reductionism of the person) that have wreaked havoc on our common history: sexism, racism, classism, materialism, etc.

Figure 4

As human persons, we are all different. We are different in terms of age, ethnicity, size, shape, color, abilities, sex, and circumstance. But how can we claim that we are all human persons, that we are all human beings? What is the being that we not only call human but that is human? It is the rational human substance that we hold in common as individuals, all having a share in this same substance. If this were not the case, no human being's dignity would be secured according to nature—according to what we are. Without reference to substance, we may very well interpret each other in a variety of less-than-human ways: illegal alien, hooker, nigger, cracker, fetus, the pregnancy, cells, retard, faggot, vegetable, problem. Substance, then, is what is not subject to change and distinct from the accidental properties, or accidents, of the individual. Accidents include all of those diverse traits that differentiate beings of the same substance from one another: color, shape, size, age, abilities, deformity, missing parts, genetic codes, etc. Without this critical metaphysical distinction between substance and accidents—between whole and parts—we inevitably will mistake the part (or parts) for the whole of a being. Reductionism (fundamentalism) haunts our thinking with a legion of counterfeit interpretations. Reductionisms betray their partial truncated interpretations of the real with language like "It is only . . . it is merely . . . it is just . . ." "God is not the author of the universe, it is only nature. Human beings are not created in the image of God, they are just complex animals. Angels are not real, they are merely an anthropomorphized ideal construct of human fabrication." The masters of suspicion—Sigmund Freud, Friedrich Nietzsche, and Karl Marx—were experts in reductionism, sadly confusing the part (no matter how significant) for the whole (especially all that matters more than matter). Instead, metaphysics prevents erroneous reductionism by witnessing to the whole of being itself and beings. Our interpretation of ourselves as human beings depends entirely on how we understand our common nature according to the common substance that makes us human.

C. Substance in the Abstract

Prescinding from this concrete example, let us entertain a few more descriptions of substance. What this example has demonstrated is that substances have determinate identities. Metaphysics also calls these determinate identities "essences" or "natures." All of this language can be confusing because sometimes the terms "substance," "essence," and "nature" are used interchangeably as synonyms. In any case, substances exist in their own right as determinate identities and cannot be predicated of anything else. Substance is the what of a being, what it is. It is a being's what-ness. Anything that is not a substance can be predicated of a substance. For example, man and woman are predicated of human and not the other way around. Other predicates of human being include young, old, tall, short, thin, stout, intelligent, strong, disabled, heterosexual, homosexual, male, female, poor, rich, etc. None of these predicates, or accidental properties, define the substance that is human, yet they all are predicated of this universal substance.

Aristotle calls such a universal substance *prote ousía* ("first/primary substance") because all other qualities and characteristics of a being are clearly tethered to and derived from this first substance. First substances are stable and immutable in and of themselves. They subsist in a being all the while the being undergoes change in its accidental properties over the course of time. For instance, the human substance includes body and soul, not as disparate parts but as an integrated whole, with the soul regarded as the spiritual form of the material body. Even though soul and body are separated (for a spatiotemporal hiatus) at death, they are integrated originally at the human being's inception as a singular nature and destined to be redeemed as such according to Christian belief in the resurrection of the body.

Yet the soul, as the person's individual spiritual (and thereby formal) core of being, is more essential to the substance of the person than the body. I could lose one of my arms in an accident and still remain fully a person because my substance did not undergo change in itself. In fact, only death enacts a fundamental rupture of integrated substantial being, the separation of body and soul, rendering incomplete what was once substantially complete.

However, through death is established a new potency of being: redeemed and resurrected being—the reintegration, transfiguration, and eternal vivacity of body and soul as one. Even during the hiatus of the rupture of body and soul at death, Catholic teaching holds that the substance of the person subsists with the soul (yet always in relation to a unique *in potentia* body that completes the substantial nature called human) until final reunification of body and soul at the last judgment. A first substance can be individuated—that is, shared among individuals—but it cannot be divided or dissected into any further parts in each individual instantiation. We have arrived at the metaphysical kernel of substance, and now must relate substance to essence and existence.

D. Essence and Existence

Everything can be peeled back from a being as predicate, quality, characteristic, or part except for substance. Substance signifies the most fundamental identity of a being. Because of substance, we understand the distinction between animal and plant and rock and star and angel and God. These are not all the same kind of being. They are different on the level of substance, at least in a generic sense. Substances are specified as species within genera of being. A horse, for example, is a peculiar substance as an individual horse, although it can be categorized more broadly under the genus animal. What a being is is determined by its substance and known by the revelatory essences that lead us to its substance. As the Persian philosopher Avicenna taught, essence precedes existence (for individual beings), just as being itself precedes beings, act precedes potency, cause precedes effect, and form precedes matter. While essence precedes its own actual existence (as form precedes matter), existence (being itself) actualizes all essences into actual being.

Substance is a primary essence because it, complete unto itself, defines the identity of a being—what a being is. Metaphysics refers to the what-ness of a being as its quiddity. Quiddity is rooted in the being's substance, and substance is the first essential what of the being. We can think of primary essences as the archetypes or prototypes of respective species of being. Also, we can think of other traits of a being that are not as essential to it in comparison with the primary essence of substance, and therefore we can think of a kind of hierarchy of essences that constitute each being. Accidental properties are more or less essential to a being.

If we take human being, once again, as our example, we can identify a hierarchy of essences. In the first place, human substance, specified by the unity of rational soul and body. This is the primary essence. In the second place, male or female. Sexual difference is more essential than ethnicity, age, shape, size, etc., inasmuch as we originate from the intrinsic polarity, complementarity, and procreative potentiality between male and female. In the third place, traits such as general anatomy and physiology that we have largely in common with other mammals, for example, being bipedal, standing erect, and nursing our young. In addition, psychological traits such as behavioral tendencies, innate inclinations, personality types, and social patterns are essential to human being in a tertiary way. So there are a hierarchy of essences that guide us toward the most fundamental essence of a being, namely, its substantial essence, synonymous with the first substance of a being. Once again, the primary essence or first substance of a being is not identical to the being's existence. Because of the ontological difference, being itself (*ipsum esse*) makes substance (*substantia*), makes secondary and tertiary essences (*essentia*) of a being (*ens*).

E. Christology

For the final section dedicated to the metaphysical concept of substance, let us make a turn toward Christology. By doing so, we will get a glimpse of how divine revelation can inform and enhance reason. Without rendering the bridge between created being and uncreated Being impossible, metaphysics achieves its full scope by virtue of receiving it from above: "All good giving and every perfect gift is from above, coming down from the Father of lights, with whom there is no alteration or shadow caused by change" (Jas 1:17). This text from the Letter of James illuminates the origin and Substance undergirding and generating all substances: divinity. Through the metaphorical images of verticality, fatherhood, and light, James signifies the metaphysical truth of the divine origin of all being. God the Father is understood best as the concealed Substance of divinity from whom proceed eternally God the Son and God the Holy Spirit. For the doctrine of God within Christian theology, we must begin with reference to the divine Substance nestled within the radical monotheism of Jewish belief: God is one (see Deut 6:4). Divine fatherhood conveys the unconditional condition of divinity in relation to the created order, as well as the intimacy yet ontological difference between Creator and creatures. As being itself (*ipsum esse*), whose primary essence (first substance) is existence, God the Father fathers beings into existence through God the Son and God the Holy Spirit.

METAPHYSICS

Figure 5

The bishops who participated in the first seven ecumenical councils were at pains to show the exact relationship between the three persons of the Trinity, in light of the incarnation of God the Son, so as to alleviate confusion and division within the universal faith of the church. What language did they use to clarify who God is, who Jesus is? The Greek language of metaphysics. Terms such as substance, essence, and person were pivotal for bringing doctrinal precision to the mysteries of faith. In particular, the Greek word *hypóstasis* secured the signature logic of Christian belief as it could mean both substance/being or person. The church's credo was perfected and coalesced around the personal unity of the plurality of substances/essences/natures in Jesus: one Person (identical to the eternal *Logos*, God the Son) with two distinct substances (one divine and the other human). At the Council of Nicaea in AD 325, the bishops professed God the Son as consubstantial (*homooúsios*) with God the Father. Likewise, we can profess that Jesus, the Incarnate Word, is consubstantial with humanity. He is fully divine and fully human, and this united plurality of identity is necessary for our salvation and the redemption of the entire created universe. If we are to be united with the divine substance into eternity, then it was necessary that the divine substance unite itself to our mutable, finite, and hylomorphic created substance called human. Because the human substance exists at the sui generis intersection of personal spiritual being and material being, the divine substance had to unite itself to creation precisely at this ontological *axis mundi* in order to redeem the whole of creation.

The logic of Christian faith sheds light on the meaning and truth of metaphysics, not only because it depends on metaphysics to express itself, but because metaphysics, in turn, is elevated by the mysteries of faith. Without reference to the question of eternal redemption—a question treated in all major religious traditions of the world—metaphysics might amount to something like making a taxonomy of passengers and cargo on a sinking ship. Instead, we behold the vital relevance of metaphysics to the measure that we raise the question of salvation, including liberation from our self-inflicted bondage in the here and now. If we want to humanize (and not mechanize) ourselves, we must think metaphysically. If we want to conduct a rational theology, we must think metaphysically. If we want to holistically comprehend ourselves and the universe we inhabit, as well as open ourselves to contemplation of God, we must think metaphysically. If we want to entertain the possibility of our eternal salvation in a rational way—one that can converse responsibly with the fields of natural science—we must think metaphysically. If we do not, we will reduce the interpretation of ourselves to matter in motion, connoisseurs of pleasure, and/or viceroys of vice who deterministically will to dominate the other since only the fittest and fiercest will survive . . . until entropy has its way.

METAPHYSICS

IV. I AM

As promised in the introduction, this book will make a decidedly theological turn to depict Jesus as metaphysician par excellence. From the biblical witness, and the witness of the living tradition of the church, we encounter a savior who is involved with the question of being. In fact, he is its answer, even if in the form of provoking countless questions that circle back to being as honey bees circulating back and forth to their hive. In Jesus, we do not find a closure of the question of being, even from the standpoint of philosophy proper. Rather, we find question opening onto question as the meaning of the answer. For Jesus, one question answered means another one raised. Jesus shows that the point of the question of being is not to solve a riddle once and for all, but to be transported by the question to encounter with the living God. The one true God, YHWH, is being itself (*ipsum esse*), but moreover, personal being itself: I AM (אֶהְיֶה; see Exod 3:14). To this day, this name of God, YHWH, is so sacred that the Jewish community does not pronounce it out loud, but rather says LORD (*Adonai*) or the NAME (*ha Shem*) in its place. Just like the question of being, the sacred name of God as revealed by God deflects closure. It radiates with a hospitality of investigation and exposure. God is revealed to the degree that God is concealed. A paradox, indeed, but should we expect anything less from eternal Being?

Before the divine name is revealed to Moses at the mountain called Horeb ("heat, fire, dry, sword, barren, solitude"), Moses confesses, "Who am I [מִי אָנֹכִי] that I should go to Pharaoh and bring the Israelites out of Egypt?" (Exod 3:11). Immediately God answers, "I will be with you [אֶהְיֶה עִמָּךְ]" (Exod 3:12a). The relationship between God and Moses is utterly asymmetrical. While Moses calls into

BEING

question his own finite and utterly dependent human being, God affirms his own infinite and paternally solicitous divine being—not merely as being itself, but being with Moses. In this unsolicited theophany to Moses, God reveals eternal divine being as Being-with. This episode of divine revelation breathes further life into metaphysics, aiding our understanding of the uncreated essence, being itself (*ipsum esse*). Not only Being, but Being-with. YHWH is the God whose being is Being-bound-to-another—covenantal being-in-relationship. The origin of the divine NAME—the tetragrammaton—begins here as response to Moses and the affirmation of interpersonal communion in relation to the mission God sets before Moses: to liberate a captive people.

God deigns to intervene because he is acquainted with the suffering of the Hebrew slaves:

> I have witnessed the affliction of my people in Egypt and have heard [*shema*] their cry [*tza-aqatam mipeneyi*] against their taskmasters, so I know well [*yada*] what they are suffering. Therefore I have come down [*yarad*] to rescue them from the power of the Egyptians and lead them up from that land into a good and spacious land, a land flowing with milk and honey. (Exod 3:7–8a)

This Hebrew biblical text is ripe with meaning in what it reveals about YHWH. YHWH is attentive to his creatures. He is a God who listens (*shema*). He knows well the suffering of the other because of his radical empathy for it. He is attuned to the face that cries out (*tza-aqatam mipeneyi*)—a face that is seen to the measure that it is heard. He condescends from his hinterland of pure transcendence and becomes immanent, Emmanu-el, God-with-us, in order to redeem his beloved creatures (see Isa 7:14). This God is interesting because he is interested in us.

METAPHYSICS

Yet the narrative goes on to punctuate the ontological status of divinity with all the more force: "I am who I am [אֶהְיֶה אֲשֶׁר אֶהְיֶה]...I AM [אֶהְיֶה] has sent me to you...The LORD [יְהוָה], the God of your ancestors [-אָב], the God of Abraham [-אָב], the God of Isaac, and the God of Jacob, has sent me to you" (Exod 3:14–15). Divine paternity is accentuated in the repetition of the word father (*ab-*) and the summative genealogy of covenantal fidelity. God the Father, "from whom every family in heaven and on earth is named" (Eph 3:15), is I AM, is being itself (*ipsum esse*), is "the Alpha and the Omega...the one who is and who was and who is to come, the almighty" (Rev 1:8), the "King of kings and LORD of lords" (Rev 19:16). God the Son and God the Holy Spirit are consubstantial with God the Father, and God the Son also is called "the Word of God [λόγος τοῦ θεοῦ]" (Rev 19:13). Jesus testifies, "Amen, amen, I say to you, before Abraham came to be, I AM [ἐγὼ εἰμί]" (John 8:58; see John 1:30; 8:28; 10:30; 17:5). Jesus's words are enigmatic. The evangelist, writing in Greek, uses the same words in the Septuagint translation of Exodus 3:14: I AM [ἐγὼ εἰμί]. Jesus could be referring implicitly to this text and the basic meaning of Jewish monotheistic faith. However, from the standpoint of Christian belief, Jesus implies this and also the theological fact that he is God in the flesh, although, in typical fashion, he leaves it up to his listeners to make this connection out of the autonomous graceful decision of their free response of faith.

Jesus is I AM manifest and proclaimed in the flesh. Jesus signals the transposition of abstract *meta*-physical truth into concrete and personalized meta-*physical* truth. Jesus signifies the necessary bridge between metaphysics and physics, between the abstract and the concrete, between transcendence and immanence, between being itself (*ipsum esse*) and beings (*entia*), between form (*lógos*) and matter (*soma, sárx*), between act (*enérgeia*) and potency (*dýnamis*), between cause and effect, between spirit (*pneuma*) and matter/wood (*hýle*), between divinity and creation. Concerning the question of being, Thomas Aquinas had a point: ontological difference. John Duns Scotus also had a (counter-)point: the univocity of being. For Thomas, we must draw a distinction between being and essence because we can abstract from every finite essence the intuition of being itself (*ipsum esse*). For Duns Scotus, we must not draw a distinction between being and essence because we only seem to hit upon being through our contact with particular essences or beings. Jesus holds together this paradox (and not contradiction) of being through his hypostatic union that conjugates in a genuine unity the divine essence of being itself (*ipsum esse*) and the created essence of humanity by becoming incarnate as a human being (*ens*) without diminishing in any way his eternal divinity.

The question of being, filled out with the questions of substance and essence, has brought us face-to-face with a theological interpretation of this question in the context of the Judeo-Christian tradition. The meaning of being itself (*ipsum esse*) comes alive with its personalization of divine revelation. Divinity is not so much a concept that we are meant to talk about, as it is persons who speak and listen to us. This marks the possibility of the metamorphosis of metaphysics into prayer. I am invited to address a personal God because he has addressed me personally. Because he calls my name—for the first time at my conception—I am welcome to call upon the NAME (*ha Shem*)—a NAME both singular (the LORD) and plural (Father, Son, and Holy Spirit), noun (Being itself), and pronominal verb (I AM). I am because God is; because God is, I am. Personhood given precedes personhood received. Inasmuch as I am a finite I am, eternal I AM preceded me from beyond eternity and awakened me into being. Moreover, because I WILL BE, I will be into eternity as beloved by God.

Key chapter concepts: being itself (*ipsum esse*), beings (*entia*), ontological difference, unity, diversity, universal, particular, contemplation, form, matter, hylomorphism, spiritual being, *sacra scientia*, *sacra doctrina*, *creatio ex nihilo*, objective spirit, subjective spirit, substance, *prote ousía*, accidents, essence, nature, quiddity, individuality, existence, Christology, ego, body, soul, *anima forma corporis*, *homooúsios*, YHWH

QUESTIONS

1. For classic metaphysics, what is being?
2. Describe the ontological difference and why it is one of the first crucial distinctions to make in metaphysics.
3. How does Aristotle's doctrine of hylomorphism help us to understand beings better?
4. What is spiritual being and how do we differentiate between objective spirit and subjective spirit?
5. What does the question of being have to do with Christology and how did the early church councils—from Nicaea (AD 325) onward—utilize metaphysics to interpret the being and personhood of Jesus?

2

FIRST PRINCIPLES

Wisdom is knowledge about certain causes and principles . . . And the most exact of the sciences are those which deal most with first principles; for those which involve fewer principles are more exact than those which involve additional principles, for example, arithmetic than geometry.
—Aristotle, *Metaph.* 1.1–2

UPON ASKING THE QUESTION of being, it quickly becomes clear that metaphysics traces the effects of being back to its first causes, as well as the logic of being back to its first principles. While chapter 3 will summarize the concept of causality, the present chapter will summarize the first principles of logic. Because of logic, we make sense of things. We know. We understand. We communicate. We encounter truth. Without logic, we could not decipher up from down, left from right, good from evil, cause from effect, or yes from no. Logic gives meaning to meaning, order to chaos, organization to parts, and purpose to life. Derived from the Greek word *lógos*, logic refers to the laws of rational thought, just as the laws of nature govern the interactions within the physical matrix of mass/energy. Logic is not so much the sum total of rational deliberations as it is the remote and cloistered light that illuminates reason. Logic is the spiritual standard of truth-telling because total self-giving is the condition of possibility for rational disinterestedness. This is to say that logic is characteristic of spiritual being since spiritual being defines free intellectual activity that orbits around invariable truth. Likewise, rational disinterestedness means that any attempt to manipulate truth according to covert self-interests is exposed and purified by the sincerity and faithful resolve of spiritual being. The common essence of all personal spiritual being as self-giving love secures and seals the integrity of truth.

With immediate reference to spiritual being, we renew the intuition that first principles are not static and empty placeholders of meaningless meaning. First principles are dappled essences of personal spiritual being that set in relief the self-manifestation of truth, not as phantasmal or delusional abstraction of abstraction, but as incarnate personhood enacted as interpersonal gift. While such language and concepts exceed the modest scope of metaphysics, we must witness (at least in passing) to the theological principle of all principles: personal spiritual being. First principles do not fashion themselves or ordain their own self-evident being. Rather, we are summoned again and again to return to divinity as the source of all contingent being, even that of the most logical first principles of being and rational thought. Ultimately, metaphysics is not merely a series of rote exercises that serves to sharpen the intellect just a little more. Instead, metaphysics is a mode of evangelization to the extent that it puts us in contact with truth—personal truth that has a face and a name, namely, Jesus of Nazareth, author of metaphysics and, therefore, the great metaphysician.

I. FIRST PRINCIPLES OF BEING

Chapter 1 already has given ample indication of what metaphysics is after: first principles of being. First principles include all that is prior to beings that are in a state of becoming (that is, moving from potentiality to actuality): being itself, cause, act, form, substance, essence, spirit. First principles are what are most original and necessary, prior by nature, absolutely unconditional and non-hypothetical. They are neither speculative nor skeptical, but are entirely necessary for raising any questions at all. In this sense, first principles are the answers that provoke the questions that lead back to themselves. Chapter 1 dealt with several first principles of being, such as form, substance, and spirit, but here we will introduce another integral concept among those that qualify as first principles: the Good.

A. The Good

Procreation. This is the law of the universe, the law of being. Begetting. Generating. Propagating. Reproducing. Being begets being begets being. How do we describe this procreative impulse of the created order? Good. What is the source of this procreative goodness if not goodness itself? Loving goodness. If we experience love and something to be good, metaphysics reminds us that this experience was preceded by a loving goodness that actualized our temporal experience of it. Edith Stein puts it well: "love is goodness giving itself away." The first principle of the Good, of course, signifies divinity. Augustine of Hippo relates that there is one and only one *res* ("reality"), namely, divinity. All the rest—creation—is *signa* ("signs") that point to the *res*. The law of parsimony does not prevent us from arriving at the divine concept of the Good. Because our question reaches that far, no partial answer will suffice. Among all the essences of created being, the Good is not an essence. It signifies the meta-metaphysical transcendence that generates beings. It is that eternal charity of sharing that elects to share being, life, goodness, and love with creatures that did not share in these eternally since they are not uncreated like the Good.

Figure 6

The Good begins to express a concept of negative theology—not in the sense of bad theology, but admitting the need to empty our concepts of their self-sufficiency when approaching and naming divinity. After all, the meaning of transcendence is that which escapes our possession, even our attempt to seize upon it as an intellectual object, manageable along with the herd of other intellectual objects. A first principle such as the Good is inaccessible directly for the intellect because it is revealed precisely by what it is not.

FIRST PRINCIPLES

As King David writes: "For with you is the fountain of life, and in your light we see light" (Ps 36:10; see Ps 80:4, 8, 20). The Good is the source and measure by which everything else comes and is measured. While not observable directly in itself, the Good is attested in its progeny of created goods. And this perpetual concealment of transcendence (by definition) preserves the glory of its goodness. "It is the glory of God to conceal a matter, and the glory of kings to fathom a matter" (Prov 25:2). If all was revealed in the same way, according to the same measure, what would happen to transcendence? It would be no more, and we would arrive at an arrested reason to stop asking any more questions, especially those bothersome "why" questions. Fortunately the Good abides in its elusiveness, allusiveness, but not illusiveness. What is illusive is the denial of the Good in the name of a lesser good that goes no farther than impersonating the Good with its sad impersonal *libido sciendi* ("lust for knowing") anything but the Good.

All this is to say that the Good is the first principle of every good. The Good, in many respects, is prior to being itself (*ipsum esse*) insofar as it is good to be, and because it is good to be, there is being. Due to the resonance of goodness within our experience of being—that it is good to be, that it is better to be than not to be—we are met by the redoubled first principle of the Good. This principle serves as the first principle for practical reason and moral life—do good and avoid evil—and will be considered in detail in the final chapter of this book. For now, however, we have alluded to an indissoluble bond between the first principles of being itself and the Good. Attuned to the transcendent contours of this intrinsic ontological bond, we are moved to contemplate not only being in and of itself, but also, and above all, the goodness of being. With contemplation of the Good comes the joyful laxative that heals the cardiologic sclerosis of perceiving being as a listless and languid threat to being.

B. That Than Which Nothing Greater Can Be Thought

What is difficult in our era is having to furnish a warrant for saying or writing the name God at every turn. Perhaps it is a matter of giving a sufficient apologetic for the reality of God before the dubious tribunal of one's own postmodern conscience. At least this is my experience. It seems never enough to prove God's existence once or even a thousand times. It is a kind of proof that must be reworked and revisited because of the nature of what it is trying to prove: that which is the absconded immovable standard of all proof. To prove something means to link logical predicates back to the substrate of predication. I say something about something because there is something about which to speak in the first place. Nevertheless, since predicates and their predicates are much more familiar and intellectually malleable than their substrates—substances—we demand that substances be converted into predicates, or else we will not believe in the veracity of substances. Yet what metaphysics teaches us is that there are objects and there are non-objects. There are corporeal atomic beings and there are incorporeal immaterial beings. First principles are among the latter. As mentioned, the first principle of all first principles is personal spiritual being—in a word, divinity. Metaphysics circulates to and from divinity. There is no metaphysics without the concept of divinity. There is no sound rationality without the concept of divinity. This is so because divinity is the self-actual condition of all possibilities (potentialities) and the sine qua non of all subsequent logical deduction. If our starting point for reason is not the first principle of divinity, our starting point will be replaced inevitably by some

FIRST PRINCIPLES

arbitrary will to power in the name of self-interest. If reason is not tethered to the NAME, it will be cuffed to some other name not above every other name (see Phil 2:9–11).

So let us pursue, once again, the NAME that supplies us with the warrant for denominating the NAME—a NAME named inasmuch as revealed—and for denominating everything else (see Gen 2:19–20). Eleventh-century Benedictine monk Anselm of Canterbury advanced the metaphysical understanding of God as "that than which nothing greater can be thought." How can such a simple statement figure so powerfully within an account of first principles? May we consider the depth of this insight? As its final word suggests, it has to do with thinking. Centuries before the time of René Descartes, Anselm is not trying to secure epistemological certainty, but is attempting to fill out his faith in God with rational demonstration. *Fides quaerens intellectum* ("faith seeking understanding").

Figure 7

As a precursor to Thomas Aquinas's rational proofs for God's existence, Anselm sets a steady trajectory that carries us even at the present moment of thought. His assertion is a metaphysical one. Contrary to the categorical misunderstanding of his adversary, Gaunilo, Anselm is not suggesting that if you wish anything wonderful, then it must exist in reality. Rather, he stakes a metaphysical claim based on first principles: if the greatest thought we can have is that of divinity (for what goodness does the concept of divinity exclude?), then divinity in-the-real is more divine than divinity in effigy of imagination. Real goodness is more good than its ideal conception and, according to metaphysics, the actuality of goodness antecedes its potential revelation and maturation within the created order of being. Anselm's ontological argument for God's existence pops according to the veracity of first principles. Inasmuch as actuality is prior to potentiality, actual divinity is prior to potential divinity—even as a concept.

Theological metaphysics involves the fewest first principles of all sciences: there is only one, namely, divinity. However, as Thomas Aquinas admits, this first principle is not self-evident because its essence (beyond essence) cannot be seized as an intellectual object like so many others, for example, heat, purple, alligator, circle, three, or smile. The divine essence is existence (being itself) and, therefore, this essence cannot be intuited intellectually. All the same, the divine essence is the first principle par excellence as it is the apodictic origin of all other principles of being and logic. Let us turn now to the fundamental laws of logic that flow from the unconditional first principle of all principles and divinity, and that govern all discursive reasoning.

II. LAWS OF LOGIC

In order to know what is real with certainty, and to communicate what is real to one another, we must adhere to the self-evident laws of logic. What is self-evident cannot be proved any further because it is the condition of possibility for knowing all those things that are not self-evident in themselves. All rational thought is based on first principles of logic, without which there would be no universal reason in which all rational beings have a share. Reason is not schizophrenic. It does not operate according to delusions and hallucinations, or according to a pure subjectivity that invents truth along the way. Reason is tethered to objective truth if rationality has any dignity, veracity, coherence, and intelligibility at all. The formal logic of right reason is not subject to alteration or revision depending on the particular local context in which it is exercised. Rather, the formal logic of right reason sets the rational standards for all thought processes that are committed to knowing what is real and true. Geometry and mathematics are examples of universal logic. A circle is a circle in Japan, Nigeria, Venezuela, Antarctica, or even on the moon. Two and three equal five anywhere in the universe because of the first principles of mathematics and, moreover, the first principles of logic. These principles are axiomatic, meaning that they are self-evident in and of themselves and serve as the immutable rules for logic. In this sense, they are substantial, not being predicated of anything else. They cannot be proved by further arguments that would appeal to some other prior principles because the first principles are in the first place. We cannot detect anything more self-evident than these. Let us consider now the three fundamental first principles of logic according to metaphysics.

A. The Principle of Noncontradiction

The principle of noncontradiction states that something cannot be both what it is and not what it is at the same time.

Something cannot exist and not exist simultaneously. A=A, A≠-A. A is A. A is not not A. Two statements predicated upon the same substance both cannot be true if the two statements directly contradict one another while they are stated in the same sense. For example, I am forty years old. This is true. I am not fifty years old. I am not twenty years old. I am forty years old. However, to be precise, I am more than forty years old, if I count the time of gestation within my mother's womb, beginning at the time of my conception onward. Then, if I add the days since my fortieth birthday, I am around forty-one years and one month old to this day. This example shows that I can state something that is true in two different senses, but I cannot state something that is both true and false in the same sense. Even in reference to both senses of counting my age, to say that I am fifty years old would be a lie—a contradiction in relation to either of the senses of stating my age.

Let us take a second example from geometry. This shape is not a circle:

Figure 8

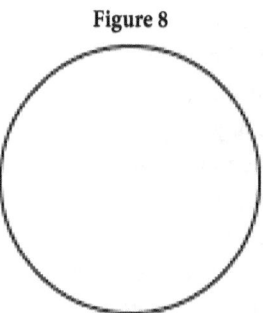

This statement is false because the shape in view is a circle. Both statements cannot be true in the same sense at the same time. I cannot say both that this is a circle and that this is not a circle. Only one of the statements can be true by virtue of the principle of noncontradiction. If I was able to say at the same time that this is a circle and this is not a circle, reason would unravel and there would be no universal grounds for making truth claims between rational persons.

B. The Principle of the Excluded Middle

Closely related to the principle of noncontradiction is the principle of the excluded middle. This principle states that there is no middle ground between truth and falsehood. With reference to metaphysical reality—the real—what is is and what is not is not. There exists no intermediate ground between absolute truth and falsehood. For example, either you are a human being or you are not a human being. Either you are an individual substance of a rational nature, or you are not an individual substance of a rational nature. Either the substance of your being is human or it is not. This substantial identity is not contingent on your age, sex, or abilities. These are all accidental (and in some cases *in potentia*) properties in relation to your unchangeable substance called human. There are not half-humans, but always full humans since the time of conception. Even in the case of chimeric adaptation, mutation, or transfer (combining genetic material or anatomical parts between human and non-human species)—perhaps more a question for future generations—once a human, always a human by virtue of the irreplaceable substance called human, a substance that comes on the scene at the time of conception, body and soul.

METAPHYSICS

Figure 9

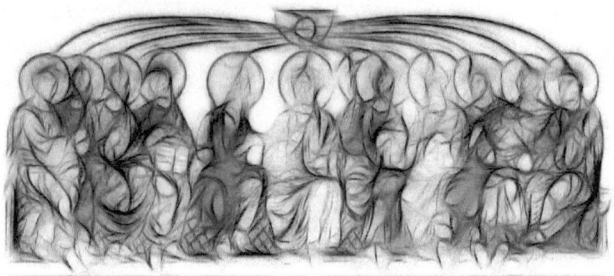

Let us invite another example from the domain of Christian theology: the Eucharist. According to Catholic teaching, the eucharistic liturgy begins with ordinary bread and wine, each substance being what it is as it is. The bread is not the wine and the wine is not the bread. Bread is bread and wine is wine. The bread is. The wine is. The bread is truly bread. The wine is truly wine. The bread is not not bread and the wine is not not wine. Neither is there any middle ground between the bread is bread and the bread is not bread, or the wine is wine and the wine is not wine. Such middle ground is excommunicated from reason by the principle of the excluded middle. However, as the eucharistic liturgy proceeds through the words and gestures of consecration by an ordained priest, the Catholic Church teaches that the substances of bread and wine, respectively, are transubstantiated into the substances of the body and the blood of Jesus Christ, respectively. The substance of bread is changed completely into the substance of the body of Jesus, and the substance of wine is changed completely into the substance of the blood of Jesus. The substances are changed radically and irrevocably. Nevertheless, the accidental properties of bread and wine remain the same (in most cases) for the fittingness of consuming the eucharistic species. Once transubstantiation occurs, the substances of the body and blood of Jesus remain. There is no middle ground between body and bread or blood and wine. They are either one or the other, substantially speaking, in reference to the doctrine of transubstantiation.

C. The Principle of Identity and Difference

Again, closely related to the principles of noncontradiction and the excluded middle, the principle of identity and difference states that what is is identical to itself and not to another. $A = A$. $A \neq B$. On one hand, there is identity. On the other hand, there is difference. These should not be confused with one another. It is essential to call a thing what it is, and metaphysics helps us to do so. An example of this principle at work is the fact that I am I. I am not you and you are not me. Each of us has our own unique individual identity, and our respective identities are not to be conflated or confused. Further, we can say with certainty that we are both humans and not dogs. A dog is not a human, and a human is not a dog. A dog will never read this book because the substance dog is not a rational substance. We can personify dogs all we want, but a dog is not a person per se because a dog lacks a rational (personal) spiritual nature.

Let us consider a second example at once sociological and theological: marriage. What is marriage, and who can constitute a valid marriage according to our metaphysical identities as human beings? Here we will discover that marriage cannot have two contradictory meanings in the same sense. Among all biological species, to our knowledge, only humans marry, since marriage involves a free rational decision to commit oneself to another human being until death. Moreover, rooted in the intrinsic differences between male and female (and the procreative potential dependent upon these differences by nature), the basic concept of marriage signifies one man and one woman bound together for life to become husband and wife, father and mother. Sexual difference is the fundamental condition of possibility for two human beings to conceive a new human being through sexual intercourse, according to nature. In relation to biological procreation, male is male and female is female; male is not female and female is not male. Both are necessary to conceive new human life. Something from man and something from woman is required by nature to welcome new human life into existence. From this standpoint, and in this sense, same-sex marriage is a contradiction of terms. Either marriage is a union between one man and one woman, or it is not, if marriage indeed is based upon metaphysical distinctions of being. Yet union—unity—implies diversity and, for human sexuality, sexual diversity refers to the intrinsic differences between male and female, as well as the complementarity that obtains therein. Male is male. Female is female. Such identities, and the difference between these stable ontological identities, are self-evident. And such self-evidence cannot be proved any further than the evidence evident to the reverent—reverent in the sense of contemplating again and again with respect and awe (from *re-*, "again," and *vereri*, "to respect, fear, stand in awe of") the question of being that necessarily involves questions about beings.

III. "IN THE BEGINNING WAS THE *LOGOS*" (JOHN 1:1)

The three basic first principles of logic—the principles of noncontradiction, the excluded middle, and identity and difference—show the meaning of first principles for metaphysics and how they function within the most basic tasks of everyday life. What would it be like to buy something from a store if customer and cashier could not agree on the difference between a one-dollar bill and a fifty-dollar bill? What would it be like to drive on roads if people could not recognize that red is red and green is green, or even that a sign that reads STOP is there rather than not there? How would it turn out in a court of law if I claimed that the stop sign on the corner of Fifth Avenue and Washington Street does not exist (when in reality it does exist)? How would it go if I petitioned that giraffes should be allowed to attend universities because all creatures have a fundamental right to education? What if I claimed that a rock had the same right as well? Such arguments made in the name of rationality are rightly deemed absurd to the degree that they neglect the first principles of metaphysics and therefore make blatant categorical mistakes.

These examples are rather humorous, but others are not. What if I refuse to call another human being human and instead use less-than-human terms such as illegal alien, crackhead, or idiot? What if I refer to an infant in her mother's womb as the cells, the embryo, the fetus, the pregnancy? What if I refer to a person in a comatose state as a vegetable? What if I refer to a woman who experiences same-sex attraction as merely lesbian? What if I refer to a person with disabilities as a retard? What if I refer to every faithful Muslim believer as a terrorist? What if I refer to a man living in prison only as a criminal? Such examples are commonplace among us, and metaphysics is absolutely necessary to enable us to call a thing what it is with accuracy and to prevent reductionistic thinking, speaking and acting. Metaphysics opens the whole truth of reality to us and not just a few of its many parts. Because of the intended brevity of this book, I can provide only limited examples of the primary concepts and thought structures of metaphysics at work. To this end, chapter 2 will conclude with a brief theological reflection of Jesus the metaphysician as the eternal divine *Logos* in the flesh.

When metaphysics meets divine revelation in a Christian key, we find that the first principles of metaphysics are not so much abstract rules for thought as they are persons who provoke the response that all creaturely rational thought is. While countless biblical texts could be referenced as a method to unpack the meaning of Jesus the *Logos* for Christian theology, I would like to allude only to the preface of the Gospel of John and conduct a short metaphysical interpretation of it. To say that in the beginning was the *Logos* and that the *Logos* is divine is to appeal to the personal Principle of all principles. For Christian theology, the eternal *Logos* is univocal with God the Son, and it is this person of the Trinity who becomes human through the collaborative *fiat* of the Blessed Virgin Mary. To refer to God the Son as the *Logos* expresses the eternal law of God that is not subject to change because any sense of the word change signifies some shadow (potency) of its resplendent light (act). In order to prevent drifting into some neo-Gnosticism, let us attend to the concrete revelation of the personal *Logos*, God the Son become flesh, Jesus of Nazareth. Again we must enter the field of Christology to observe the first principles of logic in force, especially since their force has arrived in the flesh.

Figure 10

To make a long story short, the church professes Jesus to be one person with two distinct substances/natures/essences, one divine and the other human. The two substances are united hypostatically by the singularity of personhood, namely, that of the eternal Son of God (*Logos*). Jesus shows that paradox is possible in the world of ontology, and certainly the hypostatic union of Jesus bumps up against the three first principles of logic as discussed earlier. For the church professes that Jesus is one person with two substances. Does this proclamation not violate the principles of noncontradiction, excluded middle, and identity and difference? No. If anything, the mystery of Jesus's Being/being clarifies such principles all the more. The doctrine of Jesus's hypostatic union does not contradict these principles because (1) it does not say that human is divine or that divine is human, (2) it does not suggest some nebulous admixture of radically different ontological substances, (3) it does not predicate directly something of one substance that is peculiar to the other substance, (4) it does not say both that the incarnation of the *Logos* happened and that it did not happen; it does not say that Jesus both is divine and is not divine or that he both is human and is not human.

However, by virtue of the interchange of properties (*communicatio idiomatum*) that is effected through the incarnation of the *Logos*, we are given warrant to name and make paradoxical statements about Jesus and even Mary. For example, the Son of God died on a cross, Mary is the Mother of God (*Theotókos*), the Son of Mary created the universe, the Son of God obeyed his parents, the Son of Mary is God. The distinct substantial identities of Jesus—divine and human—are maintained through their hypostatic union in the one person, Jesus, the eternal Son of God.

Finally, not only is the *Logos* divine truth, the *Logos* also is divine goodness and beauty. The *Logos* is life-giving. To encounter Jesus the *Logos* through Scripture, the sacramental life of the church, the face of the other, the bountiful beauty of creation, theology, music, and every authentically human cultural enterprise is to encounter the very source of all meaning, logic, and rationality. To encounter the resurrected Jesus as alive and active in our souls and bodies, along with God the Father through God the Holy Spirit, and to respond affirmatively to the invitation to follow him, is to build one's home—the home of one's life—on the surest foundation:

> "Everyone who listens [*shema*] to these words [*lógia*] of mine and acts on them will be like a wise man who built his house on rock [*pétra*]. The rain fell, the floods came, and the winds blew and buffeted the house. But it did not collapse; it had been set solidly on rock. And everyone who listens to these words of mine but does not act on them will be like a fool who built his house on sand. The rain fell, the floods came, and the winds blew and buffeted the house. And it collapsed and was completely ruined." When Jesus finished these words [*lógia*], the crowds were astonished at his teaching, for he taught

them as one having authority, and not as their
scribes. (Matt 7:24–29)

When Jesus the *Logos* speaks, his words are wisdom because he is divine Reason in the flesh. He compares the one who listens to and acts on his words to a wise man who builds his house on a rock foundation. In the wake of Jesus's inauguration and the subsequent evolution of the church, is this rock (*pétra*) not the Rock (*Pétros*), Peter, on whom Jesus built his church (see Matt 16:18)? Is not the sum of Jesus's words those articulated through the Scriptures and tradition of the church, including the living teaching authority of the church, the magisterium? If we can search out the truth with any degree of relative confidence, need there not be a sure and infallible means through which this truth about divine revelation, and thereby morality, is communicated to us created moral agents? If the truth of God is destined to be translated into all languages and cultures for the sake of its universal communication, would there not be a unified source and body through which this truth is dispersed to the diversified world? In response to these questions and many more like them: either yes or no.

> If you remain in my word [*lógos*], you will truly
> be my disciples,
> and you will know the truth, and the truth will
> set you free.
> (John 8:31b–32)

Key chapter concepts: first principles, the Good, that than which nothing greater can be thought, laws of logic, principle of noncontradiction, principle of the excluded middle, principle of identity and difference, *Logos*

QUESTIONS

1. Why is the Good one of the first principles of being?
2. In your own words, explain Anselm of Canterbury's idea, "that than which nothing greater can be thought," and how this idea contributes to proving the existence of God.
3. How do the three laws of logic assist us in talking about being and beings with accuracy?
4. Justin the Martyr claimed that the logos of philosophy was one and the same as the Logos of theology. How does this claim help us to negotiate between the truths of science and the truths of faith?
5. Why does the Gospel of John refer to Jesus as the Logos and how does this theological moniker shape our Christology?

3

CAUSALITY

This is how it is with the kingdom of God; it is as if a man were to scatter seed on the land and would sleep and rise night and day and the seed would sprout and grow, he knows not how. Of its own accord the land yields fruit, first the blade, then the ear, then the full grain in the ear.

And when the grain is ripe, he wields the sickle at once, for the harvest has come.

—Mark 4:26–29

CAUSE AND EFFECT. THERE are no more basic concepts than these for science. To know a being is to know its cause—to understand it as an effect of a prior cause. And so for metaphysics, to know beings is to know their common cause, origin, history, and destiny: being itself, which is the cause of itself (*causa sui*) and the necessary cause of everything else. In the previous two chapters, we have dealt with the question of being and its first principles, always implying

METAPHYSICS

the central role of causality in our interpretation of being. In the present chapter, we will recall the primary concepts of causality found in the writings of Aristotle, as well as Thomas Aquinas's uptake of these concepts within his theological project: sacred science (*sacra scientia*) of sacred doctrine (*sacra doctrina*). Finally, we will turn again to Jesus the metaphysician to discover what his life and teaching tell us about causality that fortifies and compounds our natural rational understanding of cause and effect.

You may be wondering why I find it necessary to write about such themes that have been treated at great length by other authors and so risk saying what has been said already for the ninety-ninth time. I am wondering the same thing as I begin this chapter. However, I press on toward this goal for three reasons. First, something of exceeding value is worth teaching over and over and over again. My father, John Wallenfang, was a professor of political science. When I was twelve years old, he asked me if I thought I would like to become a teacher. At the time, I emphatically resisted that vocation because it seemed to me to be rather redundant. I envisioned teaching as simply telling others what you have learned already, as if knowledge was set in stone and just needed to be regurgitated to the next generation. Instead, I hoped to invent new things, cultivate new ideas, soar to new heights, and teaching appeared to restrict pioneering new territories of discovery. Almost thirty years later, I have come to see how I was wrong. Teaching has worth in itself by sharing and serving others toward our common end (an end that is always a new beginning!) of knowledge: truth. Further, through good teaching the teacher is, at the same time, learner and perpetual investigator. Many of the greatest discoveries are made through the course of teaching. Education is a communal affair and we, as members of this

CAUSALITY

vibrant learning community, strive together toward truth and its plentiful rewards.

Second, I yearn to puzzle over what metaphysics is and the meaning of its main elements. In fact, I have written about these same concepts elsewhere and desire to write about them again as another thought experiment. With each new experiment comes greater conviction about what is the case and why. If metaphysics grants access to the fullness of the truth of being, I desire to grow in my understanding of metaphysics by presenting it to you, the reader, so that the assertions might be tested before a critical (and perhaps even skeptical) audience. If I am unable to supply a brief and legible explanation of metaphysics, then how would it be of benefit to me or to you? By composing this book, with causality at its heart, I wager that we will grow in mutual understanding of being, even if in the way of point and counterpoint, first-understanding submitted to critique and then revised to second-understanding.

Figure 11

And third, I hope to test further theological implications of classic metaphysics, much like Thomas Aquinas did in the thirteenth century. Today, however, we find ourselves in an entirely new cultural context. Basic concepts like cause and effect are not taken for granted automatically or axiomatically. The postmodern milieu claims to have graduated historically from such elementary and underdeveloped ideas. We are more interested in epistemology, hermeneutics, and contextual philosophy and theology, where we can make up the rules of reality as we go and relativize every claim to normativity. We are more interested in natural science and technology, gaining power over the powers of nature in order to shape them to our liking and vicious curiosities. We assume that because Aristotle and Thomas Aquinas did not have it all right, they had none of it right, and the same goes for things religious as a whole. Instead of submitting to these attitudes as to chains and locked prison cell doors, this book attempts a modest retrieval—*un ressourcement*—of classic metaphysics as the mainstream of perennial philosophy and the bedrock of sound theology. What does metaphysics have to do with Jesus? Everything. It is this intersection between metaphysics and Christian theology that this book intends to illuminate, even if ever so briefly. Let us proceed, then, to explore in more detail the most fundamental concepts of causality: act and potency.

I. ACT AND POTENCY

Change: a movement from cause to effect, a transition from potency to act by act. Potency is possibility, yet possibility remains only possibility (non-actual being) until actualized by an actual being. Potency is the capacity to become actual, the capacity for something to come into being or to change by becoming what it was not. Potency is nothing—nonexistent—without act. A potency cannot become actualized without act. Act refers to actual being, motion

CAUSALITY

(kinesis) or cause that makes another being become what it was not. Act is the necessary agency that brings about a new effect. Cause is act and effect is actualized being, a potency actualized. Change is the progression from cause to effect—potency actualized by the work of actual being. Potential being becomes actualized being by the cause of an already actual being:

Figure 12

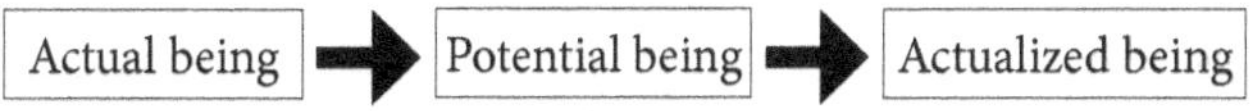

Actual being ➡ Potential being ➡ Actualized being

The basic concept of change, or becoming, permeates being like blood in our veins. In fact, the blood that circulates through our veins exemplifies the constancy of change, without which there would be no life. Change is the law of the universe, and we cannot point to a single individual being that does not change. We cannot intuit directly a being that does not change. For the field of sense perception, we experience only beings undergoing change because sense perception itself happens through change.

The only kind of being that does not change, accessible only by way of abstracting from beings, is being itself (*ipsum esse*), namely, divine Being "in whom we live and move and have our being" (Acts 17:28), "the Father of lights, with whom there is no alteration or shadow caused by change" (Jas 1:17b). And divine Being is attested only by way of analogy from the standpoint of creatures and by the self-attestation of divinity (divine revelation). For Thomas, God is *actus purus*—pure act without any admixture of potency. Aristotle asserts that actuality (*enérgeia*) is always prior to potentiality (*dýnamis*) and that from a given potential the actual is produced always by an actual thing (*Metaph.* 9.8). Therefore God is the pure actuality that precedes every

METAPHYSICS

potency actualized. If a being is in the process of change, moving from potentiality to actuality, this being is changed by some prior actuality that precedes it.

For example, it is obvious (at least to me) that I am not the cause of my own being. I did not elect to exist, yet I exist. My individual being, as a human being, was actualized by something/someone prior to me. And the same can be said for my biological parents and their biological parents, etc. No being within the universe—or even the universe as a whole that is defined by change—can claim the origin of its own existence. Existence precedes existents. This is necessarily so inasmuch as existents (beings) find themselves in a constant state of flux, change, mutation, and metamorphosis. Being itself (*ipsum esse subsistens*) is what does not change by definition because it is the cause that subsists amidst, beneath, and through all that undergoes change. Everything that did not elect to exist exists because it has a share—at least a temporal share—in being itself that was and that is and that is to come.

Being itself was because it is and will be because it is. Being itself is is. Being itself is to be. Being itself is the eternal uncreated substance that ordains and orders all of the finite created substances that substantiate beings. All diverse substances are predicates of the substance that is being itself. Duns Scotus is right to call our attention to actual essences that lead us to assert the sheer facticity of being as being (*ens inquantum ens*), being in general (*ens in communi*). Yet Thomas is likewise right to call our attention to the eternal act of being itself (*ipsum esse subsistens*), distinct from each episode of a temporal individual being, as the sine qua non for all unnecessary and radically contingent beings that change constantly. Diversity and unity. Diversity of beings and unity of being. If actuality always precedes potentiality, then being itself (in its uncreated

CAUSALITY

essence) precedes all beings (with their host of created essences). This is most definitely true, given the self-evident fact that potential being is not the principle of its own existence. Act—actuality—is the principle of every being that has actual being because the potential being of an actual being has been actualized by a prior actuality upon which its individual existence depends. Actuality—*actus purus*—is the unifying principle of all beings that undergo change. Without pure unified, uncreated, and unchanging actuality, there are no potential diverse, created, and changing actualized beings.

Act cannot be reduced to the physical concept of kinetic energy. Kinetic energy, such as that of motion or light/heat, is always itself an effect of potency actualized. No instance of kinetic energy is pure act. Even the big bang theory does not solve the riddle of what ignited the bang and cosmic expansion from point zero. From where did the mass/energy come—this mass/energy that is defined by change, laced with potency? For the entire cosmic complex of mass/energy certainly is not pure act insofar as energy is convertible into mass and mass is convertible into energy. Albert Einstein's mass-energy equivalence equation, $E = mc^2$, confirms this assertion. Energy equals mass times the speed of light squared. Essentially, this equation signifies the fact that energy and mass are mutually convertible, one into the other. Both energy and mass, and their entire network of physical being, are in a constant state of flux. Atomic and molecular polarities perpetuate micro- and macro-motion and micro- and macroevolution. The four fundamental forces of nature—nuclear strong force, nuclear weak force, gravitational force, and electromagnetic force—are based on inherent polarities among distinctly different beings, large and small. Subatomic particles are morphing constantly, one into the other. These particles are at the mercy of other particles nearby, and not one of them stays the same.

The metaphysical question increases in urgency: what gives form to the matter in a constant state of temporal flux, even at the subatomic level? What gives form to particles that constitute relations of polarity? What differentiates particles with positive charge from particles with negative charge? From whence the ontological opposition and attraction of beings, both at micro and macro levels of being? Polarity itself is not a spiritual causal agency of atomic mutation but simply a description of different forms of particles. Polarity as such does not make subatomic particles move, but the distinct differentiated forms of subatomic particles and their interaction with one another generates movement and mutation. Yet this description still begs the metaphysical question on the relationship between form and matter. How does matter become formed matter? That is to say, how does matter come into being if matter is not the cause of its own being since it is mutation itself? Protons morph into neutrons, and neutrons morph into protons. Electrons (a type of lepton) morph into photons (a type of boson) and photons morph into electrons. Heavy quarks morph into up quarks and down quarks through particle decay. When electrons and positrons collide, they annihilate one another and emit gamma ray photons. Altogether, there is no perfectly stable and immutable particle in the world of atomic physics. All is in a state of constant change and motion. And if something is in a state of change or motion, it neither changes nor moves itself by itself.

Dissecting mass/energy into smaller and smaller parts does not diminish the metaphysical hermeneutic of potency-act, but affirms it all the more. Interpreting mass/energy to the furthest spacetime borderlands of the universe does not diminish the veracity of potency-act either. Whether

CAUSALITY

physical beings are analyzed according to their smallest or largest parts, their mutable existence still begs the question of their origin and cause of change. For that which undergoes change cannot be the cause of its own change, let alone the cause of its own existence. We cannot attempt to supply material solutions for immaterial questions lest we commit yet again the fatal flaw of the grossest categorical mistake. Matter is not spirit and spirit is not matter. Effect is not cause and cause is not effect. Potency is not act and act is not potency. Receptivity is not initiation and initiation is not receptivity.

Figure 13

According to Einstein's theory of relativity, neither absolute points in space nor absolute instances of time have physical reality, but only the events of being themselves that occur with absolute relation to one another in spacetime constitute physical reality. In essence, events of being are productive of spacetime. Each being is an event of being, an absolute episode of being relative to the holistic eventfulness of being itself. Whether at the micro or macro level, being beings. The magnification of the sensory optic makes

METAPHYSICS

no difference to the metaphysical truths of causality. When we reflect on the smallness of earth in relation to the largest stars (approximately two thousand times larger than the sun) and unbounded expanse of the universe, we may be tempted to reduce our meaningfulness to next to nil. Are we not entirely insignificant in relation to the entire universe in its overwhelming magnitude? Does not the phenomenon called earth seem as random as randomness gets? To the contrary—the theory of relativity relativizes the perception of incredible smallness. Every point of reference, whether colossal or miniscule, is perfectly relative to every other one. The potency-act hermeneutic applies to all the same. In relation to being itself (*ipsum esse*), there is an equality of being and significance among beings, no matter how large or small, inasmuch as each has its own share in being. On this score, we must agree with Heidegger that Being (*Sein*) self-discloses itself through beings (*Seienden*) to us human beings (*Dasein*) who recognize the receptive mystery of this ontological epiphany. For subatomic particles, as well as for stars and planets, the metaphysical meanings of causality apply in the same manner and to the same degree. Being beings.

Being is its own event coordinator because it events itself as a symphony of manifestation. It is a privilege for me to serve as visual, vocal, and visceral vessel of this masterpiece, and I must confess that I was elected purely and absolutely (without any initiative on my part whatsoever) to participate and witness to this orchestration not my own. My flesh and bones are not my own. They were entrusted to me from an elsewhere that "formed my inmost being" and "knit me together in my mother's womb" (Ps 139:13). Methodological atheism can last for only so long, and then it is no longer interesting because, for whatever reason lacking in reason, it has lost interest in the Trinitarian Interest (from *inter-*, "between, within, reciprocal," and *esse*, "being/to be") that interested it into interesting being long ago.

Ultimately act means spirit, and potency means created matter (the non-divine par excellence) that comes into being with passive receptivity to a given form. Pure potency is the poetic canvas upon which divinity inscribes created essences of being—essences that are intertwined as one family of mutable being, but subsisting as distinct and differentiated individual beings, even if for only a fleeting wrinkle in time. There is no matter without form. Every instance of actual matter is formed matter. Pure potency is nonexistence inasmuch as it lacks actual form. Motion, too, is potency actualized—a new vector of spacetime actualized according to the event of being wherein act actualizes potency into actual being, being-in-motion toward a predetermined formal end. Every vector of motion or unfolding of being has its destination. Otherwise, no particle of being would set out on its course as on a mission to be. The itinerary of being is to be, without which nothing would be, myself included.

II. ARISTOTLE'S FOUR CAUSES

Now that the relationship between act and potency, cause and effect, has been established, let us reexamine the four different kinds of cause as related by Aristotle in his *Physics* and *Metaphysics*. By describing each of these kinds of cause in sequence, we will arrive at a more precise understanding of the relationship between act and potency, as well as that between form and matter. To this day, Aristotle presents the intellect with an invitation to think further than it tends to think on a daily basis. This is the wonderful gift of metaphysics—a gift that keeps on giving as long as the intellect is attentive to its silent and subtle apocalypse of being given.

A. Material Cause

The first and most simple kind of cause to understand is material cause. Material cause refers to the matter from which a being derives its own individual matter. Biological reproduction shows a clear series of beings that derive the matter of their individual bodies from the individual bodies of the parent organism(s), as well as the matter obtained through nutrition and hydration needed to sustain the life of the offspring. In our case, as human beings, each one of us originates from something from man and something from woman, namely, reproductive cells. Upon the fusion of these reproductive cells, our unique individual being is generated. In the case of stars, the coagulation of interstellar gas and dust particles over the course of millions of years eventually forms an individual star. The aggregate matter of stars has a genealogy traceable through the theories of astrophysics. Matter begets matter when matter is transformed into new forms of matter. Matter does not create itself from nothing. It is merely the substrate that undergoes metamorphosis over the course of time. The material cause of each material being is identical to the matter that preceded the matter that now makes up the body of the individual being.

B. Efficient Cause

Related directly to the term "effect" in its etymology, efficient cause refers to the most immediate and primary source of change or rest in a being. Efficient cause signifies the act or actual being that changes something else. It is motion or kinesis itself. It is force. It describes the presence of an actual being in act in relation to the latent potency of another actual being that undergoes change when its potency

CAUSALITY

is actualized. In the most straightforward manner, efficient causality can be summed up thus: because of x, therefore y. Efficient causality can be traced along a linear sequence of cause and effect measured by chronological time. Why are there waves in the ocean? Because of the friction between wind currents (the movement of air molecules) and surface water, as well as the gravitational force of both sun and moon in relation to earth. Why is there wind and gravitational force? There is wind due to the uneven heating of the earth's surface by the sun, causing temperature fluctuation that in turn causes expansion and movement (both vertical and horizontal) of air molecules. In addition, the rotation of the earth on its axis further affects the atmospheric temperature changes, resulting in global wind patterns. Third, humidity levels affect wind by inhibiting it (high humidity) or not (low humidity). There is gravitational force because of the proximity between sun, earth, and moon, causing a mutual attraction of solar/planetary/lunar bodies that in turn results in the movement of earth and moon along their spatial orbits. Why is there gravitational force exerted between celestial bodies? This question leads to complex concepts in physics and even different theories about gravity, whether understanding it as a physical force (Newton) or as spacetime curvature (Einstein). In any case, it is the local presence of these celestial bodies relatively near one another that generates an interaction productive of motion. Why does the sun emit light and heat—that is, radiant and thermal energy? Because of the process of nuclear fusion taking place within the sun's core, in which hydrogen nuclei fuse to form helium nuclei and release gamma rays/photon particles.

Figure 14

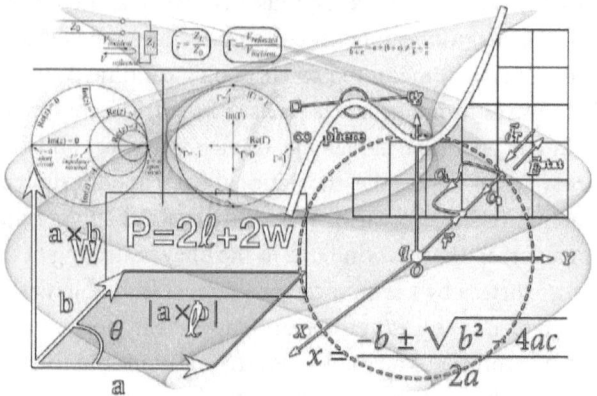

Perhaps you sense, like I do, that none of these answers are entirely satisfactory. Each question could be phrased more precisely, just as each answer could be expanded to multivolume length. Efficient causality inevitably adheres to the law of parsimony that contends that the most simple and straightforward answer is the best one because it is the most sufficient and to the point (even if a bit contrived and superficial). Efficient causality speaks to what was or what happened previously, but it does not answer why there is something rather than nothing, or why being events itself on macroscopic and microscopic scales. Why is there eternal act, and what precisely is the nature of this eternal act? Efficient causality cannot answer such questions because they clearly transcend its scope of analysis. We leave it to the following two kinds of distinct causes to entertain questions dealing with the origin and destiny of being and beings: formal and final causality.

C. Formal Cause

Formal cause is the leading cause of all causality because it is the cause that gives form to matter and the cause that gives

CAUSALITY

form to non-objects as well (such as shapes, laws of nature, ideas, and meanings). As Plato intuited centuries ago, it is the abstract formal idea that stands behind every concrete material being. It is the essential pattern according to which a being becomes and subsists in its distinct individuality. Formal cause determines not only that a being is, but what a being is. It is the act related to the potential becoming of a being in its material instantiation. Without differentiated forms of matter, no motion or transfer of energy is possible. In a word, no change is possible. Diversity of forms is the condition of possibility for the evolution of created being. Yet we ask, why is there a diversity of dynamic forms rather than only one type of inert form? What is the causal agency for the diversification of forms? I am one of these diverse forms, and I will be the first to say that this causal agency is not me! Second, this causal agency cannot be any one or few of the contingent, mutable, and transient forms at the subatomic, atomic, or molecular levels of physical being. These are radically passive particles—fragments of matter, fragments of the whole!—that depend entirely on what else is nearby to cause the change that is inherent to their ephemeral being. Why do distinct forms subsist in time—tree, rock, moon, star, water, elephant, mosquito, earthworm, fern, bird, bacterium, archaea, algae, bryozoan, mushroom, shark, jellyfish, octopus, heron, turtle, human, angel, etc.—if everything is headed toward a disintegrated physical state of thermal equilibrium with a temperature of absolute zero? Why don't we just get on with it? Why do countless forms, especially biological forms, seem to resist the natural insinuation of entropy and will to live, to subsist in their being as they are, to survive and to thrive? Why do biological beings, especially we human beings, exert tremendous amounts of energy in order to persevere in our stable, substantial, individual, and communal being? Because we rather would be than not be.

METAPHYSICS

Yet what makes me human? Why do I exist as human and not as rhinoceros, cheetah, blowfish, seahorse, orangutan, paramecium, oak tree, iron ore, lily, lion, ostrich, eagle, fox, deer, bear, raccoon, mink, mouse, beaver, salamander, snake, toad, frog, lizard, robin, cardinal, chickadee, skunk, lobster, swordfish, cockroach, orb weaver spider, yeast, bay bolete mushroom, moss, virus, amoeba, snow algae, or cenarchaeum symbiosum? Why does my individual being stay intact over the course of time and not disintegrate within a cosmic soup of atomic matter in which there are not individualized biological forms of being, let alone minerals, molecules or elements? What gives form to matter—distinct individuated forms, from subatomic and elementary particles to planets and stars? Formal causality.

Species are differentiated one from another due to the distinctive essences peculiar to each. A formal cause determines each individuated species in advance. Biological beings evolve and new forms arrive on the scene due to the formal causes that precede the materialization of each individual form, even with all they have in common. Distinct forms inhere within individual beings because of the formal cause behind each being, at times operating from the inside out (as in biological beings) and at times operating from the outside in (as in lithic sedentary beings). Matter receives form. It does not produce form from its passive, determined, contingent, and mutable status of non-agency. Mass/energy in itself is not self-created, self-formed, or self-determined because it is not a self per se. Mass/energy is completely impersonal and not free to determine itself as distinctive interdependent forms that subsist as stable ontological individuals over the course of time. If mass/energy is bent on its entropic state of thermal equilibrium, why all of the stubborn anomalies of being that resist and rebel against their annihilation and extinction of beautifully diversified and coexisting being? The essence of a being precedes and

CAUSALITY

inaugurates its existence. A formal cause signifies the distinct form or essence that causes an individual actual being to be as it is.

Figure 15

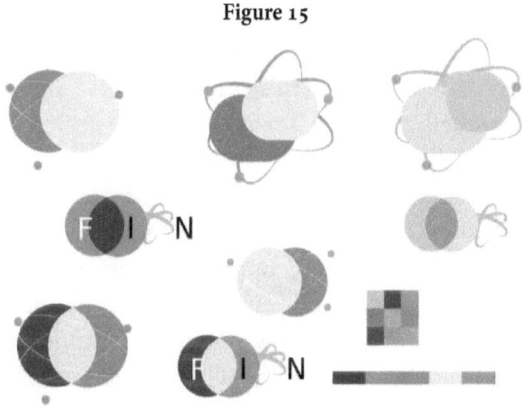

We cannot reduce the ontological identity of protons, neutrons, and electrons to their elementary parts alone (quarks, leptons, and gauge bosons). We cannot reduce the ontological identity of elements to their subatomic parts alone (protons, neutrons, and electrons). We cannot reduce the ontological identity of molecular compounds to their elemental parts alone (hydrogen, carbon, oxygen, etc.). We cannot reduce the ontological identity of anatomical and physiological cellular organelles, cells, tissues, and organs to their molecular parts alone (water, nucleic acids, proteins, etc.). We cannot reduce the ontological identity of specific composite forms of being (such as animals, plants, and bacteria in their unique species configurations) to their anatomical and physiological parts alone (hair, teeth, scales, muscle tissue, neurons, etc.). We cannot reduce the ontological identity of specific composite forms of being to themselves (as parts of a greater whole) alone. The greater whole—the whole of which all beings exist as a part—is the totality of created existents in relation to being itself (*ipsum esse*), the formal causal agency of all that has form because it has received its form from an eternal actualizing agency that gives form to matter, including that peculiar form shared among biological organisms that we call life. The form of the human body, for example, is the rational (personal spiritual) soul and if this were not the case, you would not be reading this book, I would not have written it, and you could call me a blue whale, or a cactus, or a star and get away with it. We cannot reduce the ontological identity of being itself to the sum total of its fluctuating parts because being itself is not made up of parts but instead grants all parts a share in its eternal being. Because of the clarity of the ontological difference, we can peel back the onion of being no farther. Being itself cannot be reduced even to itself because being itself involves no reduction or subtraction; only addition and attraction.

D. Final Cause

Why do beings evolve? Why does mass move (at subatomic and celestial levels of being) and convert into energy, and energy convert into mass? Is there purpose in all this motion and commotion? Yes indeed, and metaphysics gives the name "teleology" to this purposefulness of all motion and ontological interaction. Teleology (from *télos*, "end, termination, conclusion, result, outcome, goal, aim, fulfillment, purpose, forever, at last") is the science (*lógos*) of final causes and enquires into the specific purposes toward which beings move and act. Final cause is that for the sake of which a being acts. Potencies are actualized due to definite predetermined purposes. Electrons, planets, and moons orbit nucleic centers of force according to mutual corporeal attraction and repulsion. Biological organisms eat, drink,

CAUSALITY

and copulate in order to sustain their individual being and perpetuate their kind. Again, biological organisms develop and evolve in order to survive and thrive in their local environments. All that is living lives with purpose. Being is not purposeless, but is full of purpose. Moreover, beyond the realm of involuntary inbuilt teleology is voluntary teleology. We free and voluntary beings act with purpose to achieve desirable ends of action. We write and read to share knowledge, grow in wisdom, and contemplate truth. We travel from here to there with some specific purpose in mind. We invest time and energy into so many projects and undertakings in order to achieve some specific goal. When we take the time to analyze the interplay between causes and effects, we find that every cause is ordered to a corresponding or reciprocal effect. Causes cause only in light of their intrinsic effects. No cause causes without due cause to cause. Causes cause be-cause. Causes are the reasons in response to the questions that ask "why?" or "why not?" Be-cause.

Figure 16

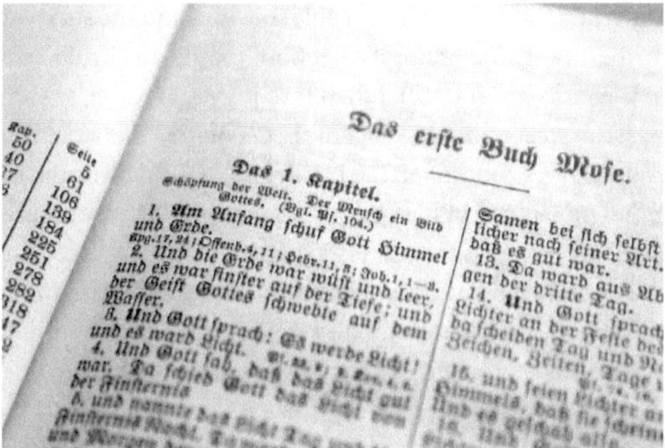

Final causes form the bookend to formal causes. In fact, we can think of them as one and the same. Form is always related to function, and function refers to the sake for which some event takes place in the realm of being. Growth, development, reproduction, movement, and even that beings exist in themselves are all the result of formal and final causality. Formal and final causes refer to the invisible, intangible, immaterial (spiritual!), and abstract agencies that generate specific beings and ordain their respective ways of being. No being can take credit for its formal or final cause. Each receives these as ontological inheritance and mission. If we are to speak of universal natures of being—such as human being (which is of great concern to us, or at least it should be)—then we must appeal to formal and final causality as the metaphysical basis upon which all physical components rest. If not, we readily can interpret ourselves away as body parts, strings, quanta, atomic particles (and their constituents), or sophisticated animals with advanced cephalization at best, or whatever else we might happen to un-call (de-vocation) ourselves.

A worldview woven from the restricted fragments of material reductionism is not able to withstand the survival-of-the-fittest and natural-selection motifs that rule in a dog-eat-dog world. What then is to prevent racism, sexism, classism, xenophobia, eugenics, genocide, dictatorships, and all other dehumanizing ideologies that rip apart the integral metaphysical meaning of human? Final cause secures the concept of universal essence in a world of becoming insofar as all beings of a common essence and origin are summoned (involuntarily and voluntarily) to a common destiny. Aristotle refers to the final cause of an evolving being or organism as entelechy; that is, the telos within the being that develops or unfolds from the inside out. The full perfection of a being is reached upon the complete unfolding of the being according to its predetermined form. However, in a world of becoming, this fullness of perfected being is approximated at best (especially for personal spiritual beings) because even more potencies remain to be actualized. The actuality of potency itself is testimony to eternal being, which delights to let potency linger into the time of eternity wherein there is no shortage of possibility, and, above all, the possibilities of interpersonal love. Perhaps we can call love the personal agency of all formal and final causes, but that notion, for all its mystery, would take us beyond the categorical range of metaphysics, accessible only by the method of phenomenology, the content of theology proper, and the mystical communion of persons known as the communion of angels and saints amidst the inner life of the Trinity.

E. Thomas Aquinas's Five Ways to Verify Divinity

At this point in the book, there is no need to give yet another apologetic that would readmit the concept of divinity into the exclusively selective jurisdiction of rational thought (especially one that insists on methodological atheism!). Nevertheless, at this juncture, I would like to take the opportunity to summarize Thomas Aquinas's five rational demonstrations of God's existence (see *Summa theologiae* 1.2.1–3 and *Summa contra gentiles* 1.10–28), based on the four kinds of causality presented by Aristotle. In our time, we look for reasons to believe rather than believe first and seek reasons later. Even though this is an exercise only in the first preamble of faith, namely, rational demonstration of the existence of God (in a purely philosophical sense, apart from any concept of divine revelation), we hazard it as necessary in light of waning belief (or concern with) God across the world due to the fact that God cannot be found among the measurable fragments of mass/energy within the limited parameters of natural science (physics, chemistry, and biology). And as a preamble to the preamble, God, by definition, is not an object among objects, a quantum among quanta, or even a being among beings. God, by definition, is otherwise than nature (otherwise than being!) because God gave birth to nature (*nascor* "to be born") and utterly transcends all beings and their finite ways of being. Let us proceed then to entertain, perhaps for the first time, Thomas Aquinas's rational metaphysical demonstrations of God's existence.

1. Act and Potency

God exists because God is the first cause of change. Nothing that changes is changed by itself, but rather is changed by something else. Something cannot be both actually what it is and potentially what it is at the same time. For example, a butterfly cannot potentially be a butterfly because it already is one. However, a caterpillar can potentially be a butterfly because it has not yet become one. For this change from caterpillar to butterfly to take place, much is needed besides the caterpillar itself; for example, nutrition and hydration and, moreover, the teleological configuration of biological metamorphosis from caterpillar to butterfly that certainly was not determined voluntarily by the involuntary caterpillar. That which is subject to change cannot be the logical cause of its own existence. Change does not cause change, but simply describes the movement from cause to effect. A cause effects change and, therefore, change (that transition from potency to actuality) is not eternal and is not being itself (*ipsum esse*). It is necessary to distinguish between primary cause and secondary causes, just as it is necessary to differentiate between being itself and beings. Primary

CAUSALITY

cause and being itself are not of the same order as secondary causes and beings. If change is produced by a series of intermediate causes, we necessarily must seize upon a first primary cause that sets the series of secondary causes in motion, and this first uncaused cause—that which is pure act with no admixture of potency, that which is not subject to change—we call God.

2. Efficient Cause and Effect

It is rationally impossible for an effect (potency actualized) to precede its cause (act) in the realm of actual being. Again, it is rationally impossible for something to cause itself efficiently—that is, for something to be its own efficient cause. For efficient cause implies a clear effect that emerges as a result of a prior cause that is different and distinct from its ensuing effect—an effected potency that has been actualized by already-existent and already-actualized being. In other words, nothing precedes itself. It is what it is and when it is because of another before it. In the seismic chain of cause and effect, to eliminate a cause is to eliminate its effect. Yet every effect gives testimony to its cause—the cause upon which it depends for its own received existence and essence. If we find ourselves betwixt a host of intermediate causes, it stands to reason that there is a first cause, and this first efficient primary (and not secondary) uncaused cause goes by the name of God.

3. Possibility and Necessity

There is being and there is nonbeing. There is that which is and there is that which is not. Something that is capable of not being, in its essence, is not. Here we encounter the ontological difference again: the fundamental distinction between being itself (*ipsum esse*) and beings (*entia*) that in themselves are not by themselves—that is, are not by their own power and initiative. Because there are unnecessary beings (beings that do not have to exist), there is intrinsically necessary being (being itself that must exist for there to be beings that must not exist). A being that once was not, essentially is not, and a being that will perish in its sustained individual existence (for all observable standards), essentially is not. So if all observable beings in the world come and go, and therefore are essentially nonbeing in themselves, we could reason that in the beginning there exists nonbeing or nothing. But this certainly is not the case with being. There is, after all, something rather than nothing and, therefore, eternally something rather than nothing. Yet something cannot originate from absolutely nothing. Every dependent and contingent being that comes and goes in its fleeting existence depends on something else. This something else that posits, holds, and sustains every fleeting instance of being in its being, and is not itself dependent on anything else, but is absolutely necessary for everything else, is called God. God is the necessary cause of all beings that could be and, moreover, must be inasmuch as God loves them from pure potential being (could be) to actual being (must be).

CAUSALITY

Figure 17

4. Gradations of Being

Every being that is expresses some degree of perfection of its essence. Every living being that grows and develops according to its innate entelechy (formal and final cause) exists somewhere along the continuum of its most perfected state of being. Embryonic forms of biological life tend toward their full development into adulthood; intellectual life is perfected through the fertile art of education; moral life is perfected through spiritual ascesis and active passivity in relation to divine grace; mystical life is perfected through the gift of contemplation and docile receptivity to divine love. All beings emerge in their individual being in relation to a fullness or plentitude of being that no being possesses on its own, by itself. Received individual being is rated in proportion to the fullness of being (*ipsum esse*) that is greater than the sum of its reflective (created from nothing) parts. If something is partially good, its goodness is in relation to the fullness of that good and, above all, stands in relation to uncreated goodness itself. If there are parts, there is a whole. If there are mutable degrees of perfection, there is an immutable standard of perfection. For being, creaturely beings exist always and only in relation to uncreated Being itself, and all fluctuating degrees of perfection—whether in terms of truth, goodness, or beauty—relate back to their transcendent source of transcendental perfection, namely, God.

5. Intelligence and Final Cause

The final rational proof of Thomas's five compelling reasons why God as such exists points to authority, rule, sovereignty, intelligence, and the inherent governance of all things. Final causality is instrumental in revealing the origin of ends. Teleology defines the way of being of the universe: all things act toward predetermined ends. Today we call these the immutable laws of nature, the fundamental forces of nature, and the laws of thermodynamics, conservation, etc. When non-intelligent beings act intelligently, this proves intelligent being behind them. Intelligence (from *inter-*, "between, among," and *legere*, "to choose, select, gather, read, speak") is the very definition of rational thought—the personal spiritual subjectivity that turns and faces every object in acts of knowledge, as well as the iconic face-to-face relationship of love and responsibility between personal subjects. If involuntary beings (mass/energy in general) act toward definite goals, purposes, or ends, it is not because they choose to do so. The rationale for acting in consistent ways must be determined in advance for change to have stable, repetitive, productive, and meaningful direction. Further, for personal spiritual beings, we strive toward desirable ends of action called "goods." The greatest good we might identify as happiness. Morality (*maiesthai* "to strive, mistress, master") is the field of study that evaluates human acts and their corresponding sources of motivation. If I do something, it is because I am motivated—moved by a perceived end of action—to do so. The one who directs all natural beings to their given ends, and who is the point of reference—as goodness itself—for all moral acts, is God.

6. I Am Received Being

In addition to Thomas's five rational demonstrations of the existence of God, I would like to add one more contribution, as inspired by the writings of Edith Stein. Stein's insight about the finite ego ("I am") in relation to the eternal divine Ego ("I AM") brings together concepts of phenomenology with the potency-act hermeneutic of metaphysics. In the last section of chapter 2 of her magnum opus, *Finite and Eternal Being*, Stein presents a persuasive testimony to the existence of God based on the reflection of our fleeting subjective life we call consciousness or the ego-life. As a person, I am. I do not merely exist, but am mindful of the existence that I am and that others (especially other personal egos) are. Yet, at the same time, I am acutely aware that I am not. There was a time I was not, and a time is coming when I will not be what I am as I am. Also, I am not yet what I will be. This much is clear to personal conscious life. Nevertheless, I am. I am a radically transient being and, without a doubt, I am not being itself. My being is essentially received being. My I am is a received I am—personally received from an eternally personal I AM. By myself I am nothing. But from I AM and because of I AM, I am. Divine I AM is actual, and my I am has been actualized. I did not posit my own existence out of nothing, nor do I sustain it over and against nothing. Someone else punctuated me into being and sustains my being at every moment.

With reference to Thomas's fourth proof of the existence of God, the ego-life is more akin to the plentitude of divine being, in comparison with impersonal beings, because its presence lasts in relation to a much greater dissipation of being than that of its own. Just as God subsists as the immutable personal stability of the instability of creation, the ego-life subsists as stable conscious agency all while the contents of consciousness remain in rapid flux. The heart of the *imago Dei* is detected here: affinity for the infinity of Being, that plentitude of personal being we call love. And this love is revealed as that "sheltering hold" of my own being—my I am—that, despite its radical transience, is sustained and held in its being from moment to moment like a child in her mother's arms. Because my being is held in being by another who is not identical to the being that is my own, I am. The one who holds me alone cannot not be. However, it is possible for me not to be. In fact, there once was a time (most of the time) when I was not. What I am becoming, I do not entirely know. If there is received being, there must be given being—being given, the cause of all beginning. This cause must be one because if it were many, one deity would lack qualities that another deity possessed and vice versa. And the one and only Deity that is, as being itself, cannot be divided into multiple beings themselves—for who would hold the being of the other in its mutually contingent being? Yet it is possible (and in fact must be actual) that there would be a personal multiplicity in this eternal unified ego-life that is the trinitarian personal substance of being itself—for who would there be to love if there was only one solitary lover with no one else to love? I am because we are; because we are, therefore, I am.

III. "WHOEVER BELIEVES IN THE SON HAS ETERNAL LIFE" (JOHN 3:36A)

To believe is to allow to be (from the Old English *lefan*, "to allow"). Within the Judeo-Christian tradition, if one believes, it is expressed verbally with the word "amen." I believe. Yes. So be it. Let it be. As the great metaphysician, Jesus is eternal life (*zoe*) in person. His being radiates the plentitude of being that saturates all impostures and counterfeits of this limitless fecundity. He is put to death by fleeting beings because of our hostility against being-more, and out of our proclivity for being-less. The crucifixion of Jesus is the tragic culmination of finite being's resistance to the vocation of eternal plentitude according to the cowardly preference for temporal ineptitude. We would rather reign supreme on our miserable islands of ego-exaltation than be sons and daughters of the King in his kingdom of other-elevation. Being becomes self-destructive when untethered from the eternal life of its nativity. Yet "whoever believes in the Son has eternal life." In other words, whoever lets being be in them, becoming "a praise of glory" (Eph 1:6, 12, 14; Elizabeth of the Trinity) oriented toward the plentitude of being that is divine, is filled with a fullness that does not originate or terminate with the self. Belief in the Son signifies a turning toward the other whose turn toward me gave birth to my being. Likewise, my turn toward the Son, whose own gaze is turned toward the faceless Face of the Father, gives being to the other who faces me to the degree that the turn of responsibility, facing the vocative face of the other, turns the earth and every celestial and microscopic spin and orbit.

As pure act, God commences creation by summoning into being that which is not God: finite being. At the limen between being and nonbeing is the potential to be, or potency. Pure potency is the radical opposite of God. Pure potency is prime matter that, without form, is essentially nonessential and nonbeing. What we call matter (which is at once formed matter) is the completely other to God. And this is why God unites this otherness to himself, without nullifying this otherness, through the incarnation of the eternal Son—through the medium of the perfectly receptive and obedient personalized (ensouled) matter, Mary, *Mater Dei*. As masterful Mother-Womb (from *maistresse*, "mistress/master," and *métra*, "womb"), Mary pronounces the perfection of passive agency, or active passivity: *fiat mihi secundum verbum tuum*, "let it be done unto me according to your word" (Luke 1:38). The life in her is the life from her because it is the life with her and for her. Because I AM is for Mary, Mary can be for I AM. As creaturely effect of the causality of the creator, Mary becomes creaturely cause of the effectivity of the creator. Salvation is effected through Mary, who was endowed with immunity from the infection of ineffectiveness, namely, original sin. Just as there must be the perfect cause for there to be any perfect effect, there must be the perfect effect for there to be any perfect cause. In Mary, the perfection of divine causality is met with the perfection of creaturely receptivity and effectivity. In this way, we can say that because of the *fiat* of Mary, God creates the universe. Anyone who utters *fiat*, even the angels, does so along with Mary. Because of the perfection of the Marian *fiat*, the divine will is accomplished in a perfect way. The doctrine of the immaculate conception of Mary articulates the fittingness that the perfection of cause must be followed (and, in a paradoxical way, preceded proleptically) by the perfection of effect. Even better, that the perfection of formal cause must be anticipated by the perfection of final cause. Only diamond can penetrate diamond, and only the perfect Diamond in the rough could woo her beloved to

CAUSALITY

the graced intimacy of incarnation. "Whoever believes in the Son has eternal life." It was the belief—the *fiat*, the allowance—of Mary that seduced heaven to earth, alluring being itself to take leave of itself alone and share itself with that which had no being, with that which had no reason to be, save for the Reason (*Logos*) that ordained its reason to recognize its Reason for being. Because of Mary, God created the universe from nothing.

Figure 18

This Reason for being is Jesus, the eternal Word of God the Father. Accompanying this Word is the eternal Breath of God the Father, God the Holy Spirit. There is no Word without Breath, and there is no Breath without Word. Neither is there Breath (power) and Word (meaning) without the One (substance) from whom they proceed. In a post-naïveté world, the miracles of Jesus are regarded as a monstrosity. They are strange and other-worldly sagas at best, and conniving and disingenuous dogmas at worst. Yet for the person of faith, miracles are inherent to the ministry of Jesus. Could it be otherwise? Jesus is the great physician and metaphysician. He can do no other than heal people of their debilitating infirmities, feed people spiritually and materially famished, dispossess people of demonic spirits and strongholds, and still calamitous storms of chaotic fury, because that is the natural—supernatural—reaction when entropy is confronted with its remedy. Since the maximum threshold of entropy presupposes its maximum opposite—the eternal plentitude of being—entropy is reversed when met with the presence of divinity.

It is little wonder that nature obeys Jesus's command, since it always is obedient to his command at every moment. The command of the *Logos* is the very laws of nature. In Jesus's miracles, it is not that the *Logos* rewrites nature, but that he redirects and empowers it toward its final cause, which is at once its formal cause: participation in eternal life. On this side of eternity, any miracle is not disclosed as a perfect fulfillment of being, but serves as an eschatological sign of perfect fulfillment to come. There remains a potency that can be actualized only through the procedure of death, which dilates the potency for eternal act to redeem the entropic decay that can be reversed by crossing out its waning deprivation. Through Son-Word and Spirit-Breath, God the Father fulfills the fulfillment of Being's fullness:

> And this is the will of the one who sent me, that I should not lose anything of what he gave me, but that I should raise it on the last day. For this is the will of my Father, that everyone who sees the Son and believes in him may have eternal life, and I shall raise him on the last day. (John 6:39–40; see also John 10:28; 17:12; 18:9)

In Jesus the Word, by the power of the Holy Spirit the Breath, nothing is lost because all is found since the foundation of being. Nothing is lacking where everything is given.

CAUSALITY

Key chapter concepts: causality, act, potency, mass-energy equivalence equation, material cause, efficient cause, formal cause, final cause, teleology, entelechy, possibility, necessity, gradations of being, intelligence, *fiat*

QUESTIONS

1. Describe the relationship between act and potency and how this relationship affects our understanding of being and beings.

2. How does Albert Einstein's theory of relativity relate to the metaphysical distinction between act and potency?

3. What are the four different causes coined by Aristotle and why is it necessary for us to contemplate being according to these four causes?

4. Explain one of Thomas Aquinas's five proofs of God's existence in your own words. Do you think that this proof is still effective to demonstrate God's existence today? Why or why not?

5. What is meant by the fiat of the Blessed Virgin Mary and why is this fiat indispensable for salvation according to Christian belief?

4

COSMOLOGY

When I see your heavens, the work of your fingers, the moon and stars that you set in place—

What is man that you are mindful of him, and a son of man that you care for him?

Yet you have made him little less than a god, crowned him with glory and honor.

You have given him rule over the works of your hands, put all things at his feet . . .

Our LORD, our Lord, how awesome is your name through all the earth!
   —Ps 8:4–7, 10

ONE CANNOT HELP BUT marvel at the magnitude of creation. It saturates the mind to think about the host of beings that participate in the eventfulness of being. Stars, planets,

COSMOLOGY

moons, asteroids, comets, galaxies, atoms, elements, molecules, animals, plants, bacteria, humans, angels, etc. The diversity of forms is astounding, and the sheer number of beings is overwhelming. Yet any true metaphysics will concern itself with all of it, as impossible as it is to do so. The true metaphysician gazes into the maze of being with gaping mouth and twinkling eye. There is no shortage of beings about which to wonder. All beings delight the metaphysician because they are charged with being. A resonance of being reverberates through the universe in which all beings are related to one another as one extended family of being. Even the physical bodies of us human beings are said to have evolved from stardust—those basic elements from which all biological life has evolved, namely, hydrogen, oxygen, carbon, nitrogen, phosphorus, and sulfur. Today we live in a different world than that of Aristotle and even that of Thomas Aquinas, both of who knew nothing of atoms; sexual gametes; the astounding biodiversity that populates earth, air, and water; and heliocentrism. Hundreds of years from now, most likely our current cosmological understandings will be regarded as rather antiquated and underdeveloped. Nonetheless, we risk an interpretation of the whole of being in metaphysics, trusting that many truths are timeless for the privileged vantage point of perennial philosophy.

METAPHYSICS

Figure 19

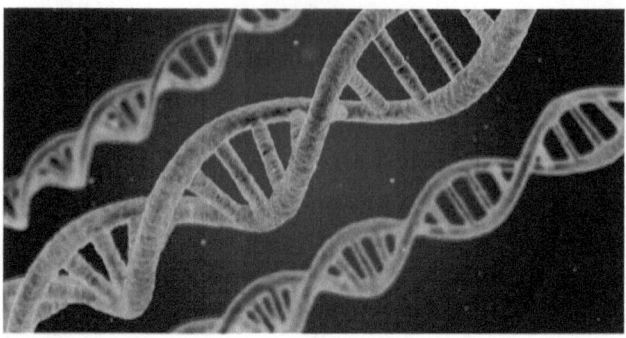

Among these truths are stable generalizations and categorizations of being as being. Concepts such as law, logic, order, hierarchy, truth, goodness, beauty, origin, end, substance, cause, and essence share the status of universality and interminability. They are applicable in every age to every instance of being without exception. Metaphysics seeks to relate the diversity of beings to the unity of being. Since there is only one existence shared by everything that exists, we are positioned to interpret all that exists according to the universal categories of being. While Aristotle identifies ten distinct categories of being by which to evaluate a particular being—substance, quantity, quality, relation, place, time, position, state/habitus, action (acting), and affection (being acted upon)—we do not intend to define and give examples of each of these in this chapter. Instead, our intention is more modest: to categorize beings according to five general orders of being in light of reason and divine revelation. In addition, we hope to explore in brief not only what is, but what has been and what will be.

Being beings with consistency. Being beings with determination. Being beings with subsistency. Being beings with innovation. In the biological realm of being, unique to planet earth (as far as we know today), there is a

COSMOLOGY

coherent phylogeny (interrelatedness and common evolution) among all living beings. This is a tremendous natural revelation that has been discovered and corroborated with much evidence only over the last couple centuries of human history. Modern metaphysics is not so naïve as to believe that there has existed static biological forms of being since time immemorial. Rather, modern metaphysics is keenly aware of biological evolution and the transient and adaptable morphology of organisms in relation to their respective environments. Metaphysics is not unaware of the symbiotic network of biological life that altogether forms macro-level ecosystems and the collective biosphere of earth. All of the most current knowledge of evolutionary biology and astrophysics (at least in general terms) will be taken into account throughout this chapter.

All the same, metaphysics invites the fields of natural science to think according to a bigger picture of ontology than only random matter in motion that just so happens to take the form of a penguin, a moose, a human, or a peacock. Material and efficient causality remain tethered to formal and final causality. If living forms evolve, it is because they evolve toward predetermined ends in relation to specific functions and purposes. Fish have fins and gills to swim and to respire within water. Birds have wings to fly, and the function of flight enhances their ability to prey, forage, and migrate, as well as to flee predators. Similarly, all biological organisms have adapted anatomically (form) so as to perform physiologically (function) and thereby survive and thrive. However, it is the universal laws of nature that set the common physical patterns according to which all beings (biological or otherwise) are subject and accountable. May we continue our metaphysical analysis of the universe by reflecting on the universal concepts of law and order.

METAPHYSICS

I. LAW AND ORDER

There is cosmos ("order") and not sheer chaos ("disorder"). For there to be any disorder, there first must be order and organization to dis-order and to dis-organize. Once again, the inertia toward maximum entropy (disorder) implies the minerva ("intelligence") of its maximum opposite (order). Even within a universe prone to depravity, deprivation, and decay, we find exquisite order and harmony. That there is life on earth—this seemingly happenstance planet within this serendipitous solar system in this incomprehensively vast expanse of stars and galaxies—tickles the contemplative mind. Cosmos and not chaos. The immutable laws of nature govern the interaction of beings. Grounding the four fundamental forces of nature and all of the laws of physics are even more fundamental metaphysical concepts: unity and plurality, attraction and polarity, same and other, as well as motion, light, heat, and relationality. Metaphysics does not take such concepts for granted or as incidental to science, but regards them as foundational to all interactions among the beings that comprise the universe.

What is? Being and beings. How are they? In relation to one another. Attraction and repulsion. Homeostasis. Inertia. Friction. Velocity. Resistance. Momentum. Symbiosis. What do I have to do with the farthest star from earth? Everything. We both have being, and inasmuch as we both have being, we have something to do with one another. Distance and proximity are relative for being as being. Everything is fair game for metaphysics, and there is not one being with which it is unconcerned. Cosmology considers the order of the universe in its saturating totality, and the first point of recognition for metaphysical cosmology is that there is a cosmos and not utter chaos. This cosmos is ordered brilliantly according to its inherent laws that serve

COSMOLOGY

the intentions of formal and final causality and, more precisely, the intentionality of divinity. Even more interesting than the laws of physics are the moral laws that originate with God and are the living architecture of all personal morality. These will be treated in the final chapter of this book, but for now, let us ponder the five general orders of being that inhabit (and transcend) the universe.

II. HIERARCHY OF BEING

A term coined by Dionysius the Areopagite in the sixth century, hierarchy refers to sacred orders of being (from *hierós*, "sacred," and *arché*, "principle, power, basis, origin, prime"), both celestial and ecclesiastical. In fact, for the theological imagination of Dionysius, the sacred orders of the church reflect the orders of cosmological being. An unfortunate homophone occurs in the English language with the word hierarchy, as it is heard as "higher-archy," giving the impression that it refers to various ranks or classes of beings ranging from higher to lower. While there is some truth to this homophonic meaning, the essence of the term as applied anthropologically connotes equality of dignity and worth, yet differentiation of role or function within the community. It is the difference between envisioning hierarchy as a pyramid or as concentric circles:

Figure 20

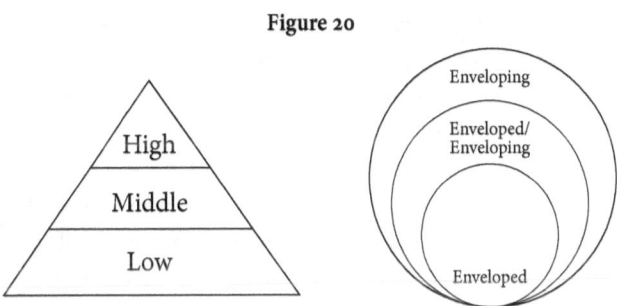

METAPHYSICS

There is a tendency to think the pyramid model and social stratification upon hearing the word "hierarchy." This image conjures up the common experiences of inequality, domination, belittlement, oppression, exploitation, vulnerability, and the abuse of power. It is a fitting image for the historical trends of social stratification into three distinct economic classes—aristocracy, bourgeoisie, and proletariat—or even a clericalist concept of the church with clergy (pope, bishops, priests, and deacons) ranked as having highest dignity and power, and the laity ranked at the bottom of the pecking order and tasked with the threefold mission: pray, pay, and obey.

However, the Dionysian notion of hierarchy signifies much more the image of concentric circles in which responsibility increases in proportion to power. In this model, the purpose of power is to serve and to share it. The purpose of power is to empower the other, to raise the other up, to ennoble the nobility of the other that is already innate to his or her being. If one has a greater share of power in relation to another, the relationship is defined by care and responsibility, expressed through the image of envelopment. Just as a mother envelops her child in her womb, creative ontological power works the same. Power serves its purpose to the degree that it is put at the service of the other who faces me. It does not exist in order to be hoarded and to insulate the self, or to exploit the other in his or her weakness. Hierarchy, therefore, indicates a differentiated, united, symbiotic, and complementary nexus of being, rather than a homogeneous, divided, unrelated, or dissociated randomness of unbecoming.

Dionysius is led by the example of Jesus, who demonstrated the greatest potential of power: "the Son of Man came not to be served but to serve, and to give his life as a ransom for many" (Matt 20:28). This is the crimson thread of the great chain of being: to live so as to die so as to give life. Whether stellar or biological creatures, all are conceived and born so as to die, and thereby share their being with new beings. Both predation and parasitism reveal this general rule of being among biological organisms. Nutrition and hydration are natural processes that transform one kind of being into another. The disintegration of one being is at the service of the reintegration of another. Light and life are paradoxical. To the measure that the star shares its light, it dies but another lives (as the expanding supershell of a supernova initiates a new generation of stars, or as photosynthesis is conducted by plants and some bacteria and protists, or as phototrophic archaea use sunlight as an energy source). To the measure that an organism expends its energies in its vital processes (growth, development, reproduction)—even all the way to abandoning its own life (voluntarily or involuntarily) for the sake of another—it dies but another lives. For biological beings, death marks the transition from an animated body to an inanimate corpse. The corpse, however, naturally decomposes, and its elements are diffused into the local environment or consumed by other organisms. The greatest proportion of biomass on earth is composed of microbial life—archaea, bacteria, and protists. These inhabit just about every crevice of the planet, and many of them feed on organic compounds that emerge upon the decomposition of larger organisms. Within the symbiotic orders of being, nothing is wasted or lost because all is transformed.

Yet in spite of the radical transience of both animate and inanimate beings, distinctive species of being subsist, even if for rather short periods of time. Geology unearths a wealth of lithic forms—for example, igneous, sedentary, and metamorphic rocks, in addition to other minerals, soils, sediments, and fossils. Biology uncovers a multitude of symbiotic lifeforms, classified according to three domains: archaea, bacteria, and eukarya (classified further into four kingdoms: animals, plants, fungi, and protists). Astronomy, too, showcases an abundance of celestial forms: stars, planets, moons, gases, ice particles, black holes, comets, and asteroids. The periodic table of elements and microphysics unveils a horde of miniscule particles that make up all larger conglomerate masses and specific macroforms of being. Then, in the realm of pure spiritual beings, we index angels, demons (fallen angels) and divinity. All species of being can be categorized according to the following five orders of being: divine being, angelic being, human being, biological being, and elemental being. The following image of concentric circles communicates the interrelatedness of these orders of being through the image of womb, with each order of being enveloping the next.

Figure 21

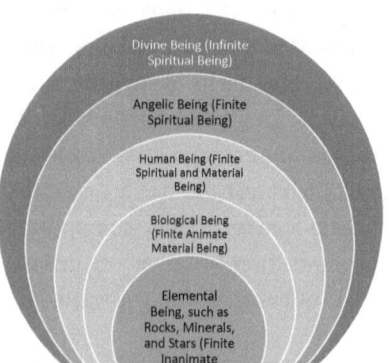

Though the ontological difference obtains between divinity and creation, this depiction of being follows Duns Scotus's insistence on the univocity of being in order for theology and natural science to have something to say to one another. Without the concept of the univocity of being, all things theological or religious may have to remain sidelined from candid public discourse about what is. However, I employ the concept of the univocity of being under the provision that we refer to God with ontological categories only by way of analogy (*analogia entis*) and, therefore, what we predicate of God, we always do so, neither univocally nor equivocally, but analogously.

Without defining and describing each of these five orders of being at length, it suffices for our purposes to note their distinction, collective genealogy, and complementarity. What is held in common among them is a matrix of mediation. All inner circles mediate divine creativity and communication in hierarchical fashion. Each inner circle of being represents a distinct yet mutually dependent relationship with the circle(s) of being within it. According to the cogent distinction of ontological categories—for example, infinite spiritual being, finite spiritual being, finite spiritual and material being—an angel is not only a speculative type of creature, but a necessary one by virtue of the actual ontological category that must obtain in between divine infinite spiritual being and human finite spiritual and material being. Ontologically speaking, because pure finite spiritual beings are possible, they must be actually, given a metaphysical cosmology composed of a hierarchical gradation of being. Actuality is always prior to potentiality, and metaphysical cosmology secures the veracity of divine being and angelic being inasmuch as spirit is distinct from matter, act is distinct from potency, and persons are distinct from nonpersons.

Angels mediate divine *creatio ex nihilo* ("creation from nothing"), *creatio continua* ("continuous creation"), and *creatio redemptio* (the process of cosmic redemption). Just as suitable and proportionate conductors channel electricity from higher to lower concentrations of delocalized electrons, or higher to lower gradients of potential energy, angels serve as necessary, intermediate, pure, personal, spiritual beings between divinity and humanity. Without such mediation, the direct unmediated force of divinity would be too overpowering for humans who exist at the intersection of fallen personal spiritual and material being. As angels are stewards of humans, humans are stewards of one another and of the entire biosphere of earth and beyond. We exist in a relationship of responsibility, not just for ourselves, but for all. Like angels, the human being is the responsible being—agent responsible—who exercises a power of care and cultivation in relation to the rest of the natural orders of being. As personal creatures with rational souls, we turn and face the natural world as habitat and home. We produce tools, machines, textiles, and synthetic polymers to enhance the efficiency and ease of our daily tasks. We harness the inbuilt powers of nature to create vaccines, medicines, diagnostic techniques, and surgical procedures to promote health. We extend the reach of our transportation through land, sea, and air. All that we do to transform nature (for good or for ill) can be condensed into a single word, namely, culture. We are beings of culture and responsibility, interacting with one another and within our environment as privileged beings found at the crux of personal, spiritual, and material realms of being.

The concentric circles above follow Aristotle's delineation between vegetative souls, sentient souls, and rational souls. The adjective "spiritual" is reserved for persons, while the adjective "animate" (related to the Latin word for "soul," *anima*) is applied to nonpersonal vegetative and sentient biological beings. The adjective "inanimate" is applied to non-biological elemental being, since it is not animated from the inside out and neither grows, develops, nor reproduces according to an inner living entelechy. In contrast, all biological beings have life (*bios*) because they are animated from the inside out; however, only humans have rational souls and life (*zoe*)—in addition to biological animation and being fashioned in the *imago Dei*—and therefore are ontologically distinct as persons within the biological realm of being. Though all matter, and moreover all biological being, is caused by spirit in terms of formal cause, the language of spiritual being in Figure 21 implies the peculiar identity of personhood expressed in rational agency, freedom, intellection, responsibility, and self-donating love. This is, properly speaking, the realm of spirit as persons human, angelic, and divine.

III. THE TRANSCENDENTALS

Personal spiritual beings do not deal only with things as objects of knowledge, but with the relationships that transpire between the person and every encounter with being and beings. Whenever being and beings are met in their reality, and not obscured or distorted through some reductionism or illusion, we call this authentic reception of the saturating fullness of being true, good, and beautiful. These three ideas beyond the general categories of being—such as substance, quantity, quality, and place—are called transcendentals because they transcend such categories, have universal application, and bear the character of transcendence within human experience. Experiencing truth, goodness, and beauty testifies to a whole greater than any one or sum of its parts. Only a personal ego (I am) witnesses to these transcendentals because they are what provoke and accompany our quest for being. We only raise the question of being at all because it is a question at once true, good, and beautiful. We make evaluative judgments about being and beings always in relation to these transcendental standards of value. Truth is the transcendental standard for judging objects of knowledge. Goodness is the transcendental standard for judging objects of conation or moral striving. And beauty is the transcendental standard for judging objects of satisfaction or fulfillment.

The triad of transcendentals originated with Plato, not in a systematic presentation, but with a distinguished emphasis that puts truth (*alétheia*), goodness (*to agathón*), and beauty (*kalos*) in sharp relief against all other minor concepts in comparison. The transcendentals are the *pièces de résistance* of eros—that ardent desire that yearns with all its might for what alone can satisfy the disquieted soul. Metaphysical cosmology attends not only to the partitioned orders of being that compose the universe, but also to the irreducible standards of evaluation that serve as the formal and final erotic causes of being. Truth, goodness, and beauty are the three fundamental forces of subjective being insofar as they propel us toward our ultimate ends of logic, morality, and aesthetic discernment.

IV. ESCHATOLOGY

Our experience of the transcendentals in this life attests to an eschatological rendezvous in their company. Eschatology—an investigation of the final frontiers of being, in light of questions about its origin and history—completes an inclusive cosmology by exploring the concept of final causality on a cosmic scale. What do the natural sciences tell us about the end of the universe? The wages of entropy is thermal equilibrium: a comprehensive chaotic disintegration of being to an incredibly low temperature (-273.150 °C, or 0 °Kelvin, absolute zero!) at which there is virtually no diversification of being into various species and, it goes without saying, no biological life. How does this translate in terms of morality? "The wages of sin is death" (Rom 6:23a). Sin is the theological meaning of moral entropy—an unraveling of being and relationships due to a drift from the Good. As much sin, as much death. According to the law of entropy, in the end, death.

In spite of this metanarrative of total destruction and devastation, there is life for now. Yet if there is life now, then, in the beginning, life. Act precedes potency. If the eternal Act is living, then it stands to reason that, in the end, life. The causal agency that gave rise to life in the first place is the same causal agency that will restore life in the last place: "but the gift of God is eternal life in Christ Jesus our Lord" (Rom 6:23b). Why not cut right to the chase? In the end, resurrection, because, in the beginning, life. Here again is where reason and divine revelation coincide. It makes no sense to claim that, in the beginning, no-life, because, in the end, no-life. Even natural science admits that, in the beginning, there was a big bang and not -273.150 °C. The dying universe is the infected effect of an undying cause and, therefore, the universe is charged with the potential to disinfect and to resurrect. This would be nothing less than the holy inversion of chaotic entropy, reinstating the cosmos that was meant to be cosmos (ordered being) from the beginning of creation. Jesus's resurrection from the dead is entropy inverted. In fact, every person that Jesus speaks with, heals, encourages, inspires, and forgives is entropy inverted. The glorious lives of the saints give ample witness to the truth, the goodness, and the beauty of resurrected life. This gift of eternal life, about which Paul of Tarsus testifies, is a gift that is received to the measure that it is given away.

METAPHYSICS

V. "THE REDEEMER OF MAN, JESUS CHRIST, IS THE CENTER OF THE UNIVERSE AND OF HISTORY" (JOHN PAUL II, REDEMPTOR HOMINIS, 1)

The subtitle of this book, *A Basic Introduction in a Christian Key*, neither attempts to conceal nor is ashamed of the complementarity and mutual enrichment of reason and revelation, of philosophy and theology. Again, as a theologian, I cannot prevent my mind (intellect) and heart (affectivity) from turning toward things theological. Perhaps in this way I am a bad philosopher, and some even may say that I am a bad theologian. It makes no difference to me: "It does not concern me in the least that I be judged by you or any human tribunal; I do not even pass judgment on myself... the one who judges me is the Lord" (1 Cor 4:3–4b). All I know is that I am compelled to witness to the truth, goodness, and beauty that I have encountered on this side of eternity, and Jesus, the *Logos*, through his incarnation, makes these transcendentals immanent. With reference to Jesus, the three transcendentals are not so much ends in themselves as they are witnesses to him. All truths, all goods, and all that is beautiful points to Jesus as their source and summit. For what is more true, good, and beautiful than God becoming flesh for our salvation, not only as an idea (indeed there is no greater thought!), but above all as revealed in history and encountered in person through the living tradition (*parádosis*) of the church?

As the Alpha and the Omega, Jesus is the beginning and end of all being and beings (see Rev 1:8; 21:6; 22:13; Isa 41:4; 44:6). He is the eternal God revealed in the physical and material intimacy of flesh and blood. By uniting creation to himself hypostatically, God ushers in the redemption of the cosmos. Resurrection is not only an anthropological

COSMOLOGY

phenomenon, but a cosmological one. However, anthropology is the pivotal axis of cosmology since human beings unite the integral realms of personal spiritual being and material being. This is why God becomes human: love limited for the sake of love. The caducity of being is overcome by the immunity of Being. Trust in the redemption won by Jesus is, at the same time, trust in the Being (pronominal verbal *ipsum esse*) that upholds the feebleness and frailty of my being (pronominal accusative *ens*). By becoming human, the eternal Son of God appears to limit the prerogatives of eternal Being unlimited (infinite). But through this paradoxical self-limitation, the potencies of divine love are redoubled. Because love is put to its greatest test in suffering as forbearance, endurance, and perseverance, divine love is able to express its unlimited horizon of Being all the more eloquently and persuasively. It is one thing to be without limits. It is another thing to be without limits precisely in and through limits. In the end, limitation is no limitation when divine delimitation delimits it.

"Jesus Christ is the same yesterday, today, and forever" (Heb 13:9). Divine love is unconditional. There is nothing you can do to make God love you more, and there is nothing you can do to make God love you less. Divine love is contingent on nothing that we think or do not think, say or do not say, do or do not do. It is determined entirely by divine initiative and is the reason for our being. I am because I AM. If the divine intentionality of Being turned away from me for an instant, I would cease to exist. Instead, "by the grace of God I am what I am, and his grace to me has not been ineffective" (1 Cor 15:10a). I am what I am because "I am who I am" (Exod 3:14a). Thomas Aquinas suggests that the reason for such diversification of being in the universe is that this diversification allows divinity to manifest its plentiful glory all the more. The universe has

METAPHYSICS

evolved according to the splendor of divine formal and final causality, and will continue to evolve through an ecstatic inversion of entropic decline into eternity. There has been a fall in being, at once moral and ontological, and this fall itself has become the potency of its redemption. No act could accomplish the actuality of redemption save for the divine Act—in two Acts: Act 1 (creation) and Act 2 (redemption)—whose protagonist is Act itself in the flesh.

Figure 22

Cosmology remains cosmology (from *kósmos*, "order," and *lógos*, "rational, ordered word") and not nihilistic chaos, because Jesus is the *Logos* of the cosmos. How can we explain the cosmos without reference to Christ? This would be like trying to measure and calculate without numbers. Jesus is the logarithm of being, created and redeemed. As truth, goodness, and beauty in person, Jesus is the Object, at once Subject, who gives rise to a world of objects and subjects. As truth, he is "the love that surpasses knowledge" (Eph 3:19), and "the peace of God that surpasses understanding" (Phil

4:7), in relation to whom "I even consider everything as a loss because of the supreme good of knowing Christ Jesus my Lord" (Phil 3:8a). I know Jesus inasmuch as I am known by him, for "knowledge inflates with pride, but love builds up ... if one loves God, one is known by him" (1 Cor 8:1, 3). Truth is revealed in Jesus as the unconditional love of divine intimacy from which nothing can separate. There is nothing more certain than this.

As goodness, Jesus is the apophatic witness to a goodness that grows in proportion to humility, self-denial, and solicitude for the other: "Why do you call me good? No one is good but God alone" (Mark 10:18). Goodness expands to the measure that it is deferred in reference to God the Father, the giver of all good gifts: "All good giving and every perfect gift is from above, coming down from the Father of lights, with whom there is no alteration or shadow caused by change" (Jas 1:17). I encounter the fullness of goodness when I relate every created good to the uncreated Good, even as I hear the uncreated Good say to me "very good" (Gen 1:31b) and "well done, my good and faithful servant" (Matt 25:21a). All conation, or striving, is tethered to the uncreated Good as a canopy to its apogee. Goodness is revealed in Jesus as the disinterested love of the Good. There is nothing more praiseworthy than this.

As beauty, Jesus is the manifest and proclaimed "beauty of the LORD" (Ps 27:4c), "the branch of the LORD [that] will be beauty and glory" (Isa 4:2), "a beautiful diadem for the remnant of his people" (Isa 28:5b), "the King in his beauty" (Isa 33:17). In turn, the beauty of Jesus is a beauty multiplied by a beautiful message sent by a beautiful messenger: "How beautiful upon the mountains are the feet of the one bringing good news, announcing peace, bearing good news, announcing salvation, saying to Zion, 'Your God is King!'" (Isa 52:7; see Rom 10:14–17). The beauty of Jesus proliferates as he "makes everything beautiful in its time" (Eccl 3:11a), including you and me. Beauty is revealed in Jesus as the satisfaction and fulfillment of every desire, save none. All yearning is quenched by the desert springs of the beauty that is Christ, who not only grants me being but calls me beloved: "you are precious in my eyes and honored, and I love you" (Isa 43:4a), "I belong to my beloved, and my beloved belongs to me" (Song 6:3a). There is nothing more desirable than this.

<u>**Key chapter concepts:**</u> cosmology, evolution, cosmos, chaos, hierarchy, transcendentals (truth, goodness, beauty), eschatology

QUESTIONS

1. What is cosmology and why does it hold a central place within metaphysics?

2. What is the meaning of the word "hierarchy" and how does this concept help us to organize the diversity of beings of which the universe is composed?

3. How can we demonstrate the existence of angels within a metaphysical hierarchy of being?

4. What are the three Platonic transcendentals and what do these have to do with human desire?

5. What does eschatology have to do with cosmology and how does the resurrection of Christ alter our cosmology according to the metanarratives of physics?

5

MORALITY

I call heaven and earth today to witness against you:
I have set before you life and death, the blessing and the curse.
Choose life, then, that you and your descendants may live,
by loving the LORD, your God, obeying his voice and
  holding fast to him.
  —Deut 30:19–20a

And your ears shall hear a word behind you:
"This is the way; walk in it," when you would turn to the
right or the left.
  —Isa 30:21

Though rather abbreviated, chapters 1–4 of this book have attempted to foster a contemplative metaphysical interpretation of the world. The façade of popular culture has been unmasked and punctured by the contemplative gaze toward being. One final step remains: a turn toward morality. Upon contemplating being and beings in the fullness of their being, a pestering question lingers. So what? What does metaphysics have to do with morality and daily living? Does it go beyond a deeper appreciation of being and speak to practical ethical situations? Yes. Metaphysics serves as foundational to moral life in addition to rational thought. Because it is the science of first principles, metaphysics is necessary for any claims to universality and absolute moral norms. Without metaphysics, we are left to tread water in a sea of moral relativism with no land in sight. There is no sound ethics without metaphysics because morality precedes ethics and the Good precedes morality. As the science of the Good and its first principles, metaphysics substantiates that which is worth striving after.

Just as physics detects the causes of motion in the natural world, metaphysics ascertains the causal motives of human action in relation to a working concept of the Good. Everyone acts toward some idea of the Good, whether consciously or subconsciously, whether admitted or not. We do what we do—even if giving in to the inertia of a couch-potato life—because we are moved toward the Good. Acts of the greatest violence, destruction, and evil also involve some intentionality in the direction of the Good, although perceived according to a corrupted or distorted concept of it. Morality (*maiesthai* "to strive") implies striving after the Good, and the evaluation of human moral acts is based on a clear and cogent understanding of the Good. This itself is wisdom. The wise person is acquainted intimately with the Good in all its truthfulness and beauty because s/he seeks after it and contemplates it with the goodness that is his or her intellectual and mystical being. The demarcation between virtue and vice is determined by the Good. The contrast in character between the sinner and the saint (a sinner become saint by divine grace) is deciphered by the Good.

The spectrum between the fullness of being and nonbeing is delineated by the Good.

The Good—divinity, the eternal plentitude of being—is the premier metaphysical concept for morality. Without the concept of the Good, there is no striving, not even for the involuntary events of the physical order of being. Without the Good, there would be no formal or final causality (let alone material and efficient causality), for it is good to be, to be alive, to strive, to survive, and to thrive. Motion itself is motivated by the emotive personal affectivity of the Good who wills beings into being because it is good for them to be. The Good is the zero point of orientation for all moral reasoning. It is the sine qua non point of reference for all moral evaluation and judgment. Something is morally good or evil only with reference to the Good. Personal subjectivity is rooted in the personalism of the Good who shares the goodness of being not only with other beings as such, but also, and more specifically, with personal spiritual beings capable of intuiting the Good and in turn sharing the Good according to the pattern of its generous self-diffusion. Keeping this preface to the Good in mind, let us turn our attention to the metaphysical first principle of morality.

I. DO GOOD AND AVOID EVIL

While the first principle of theoretical reason is the principle of noncontradiction, the first principle of practical reason is to do good and avoid evil. There is nothing more self-evident than this in the field of moral reasoning. If we strive after anything, is it not good? Is not goodness synonymous with the goal toward which a moral agent strives, including the goodness of the act of striving itself? If the dividing line between good and evil is the pivotal point of moral discernment, how are we to describe what is good?

Even though the first principle of morality, do good and avoid evil, is self-evident as a first principle, clearly discerning the good as good is not always self-evident. How might we describe what is good? What is good promotes the holistic well-being, health, and flourishing of individuals and communities. Goodness is related directly to truth and beauty. Does an act accord with what is metaphysically true about being and beings? If yes, then it is a good act. Does an act accord with what is metaphysically beautiful (meaning comprehensively fitting, fulfilling, and satisfying) about being and beings? If yes, then it is a good act. In other words, does an act respect the exigencies and integrity of being and beings? Is the act at the service of human dignity and the common good? Does the act adhere to the self-evident ontology of creatures in their totality of being? Does its end justify its means, and are its means in keeping with the integrity of its end? These are the kinds of questions that metaphysical thinking asks in approaching specific moral dilemmas.

A second point of reflection is the concept of evil. If we have a definite sensibility toward the Good, then what is meant by evil? For classic metaphysics within a Judeo-Christian framework, evil as such lacks a real essence because it describes a lack of goodness by definition. Evil in itself is nothing. Its concept registers to thought only in relation to goodness, precisely as a deprivation of goodness. There is no force of evil. There is no substance of evil. There are no essential properties or predicates of evil that would rival those of the Good. As being itself (*ipsum esse*), the Good is everything and lacking in nothing. Evil simply indicates less good than could be in a given being or in a given situation. Light is the perfect analogy with which to compare the relationship between good and evil. Darkness is merely an absence of light. It is not its own physical entity,

MORALITY

as opposed directly to light. Darkness is the visual state of affairs when light is absent either by its lack of presence or its obstruction, thereby casting a shadow. Evil, long before signaling moral turpitude, signifies a lack of fullness and an affinity or resemblance of nonbeing. In this sense, all of creation is evil (lacking) in relation to the uncreated Good (lacking nothing). All creation emerges from nonbeing and, therefore, is forever related to it. Likewise, in this sense, all potency is evil insofar as it stands in need of the goodness of actual being to actualize it into being. Nevertheless, all creation and all potencies are good insofar as they have been given a share in being by the Good (see Gen 1:4, 10, 12, 18, 21, 31).

Figure 23

Once our moral compass is calibrated according to the Good, and we have gained sufficient familiarity with the concept of its lack (evil), we can proceed to examine the second fundamental principle for human morality: the personalistic norm. The principle of the personalistic norm was coined by Karol Wojtyła in his 1960 book *Love and Responsibility*. Combating the utilitarian tendencies of modernity, Wojtyła put a personalist spin on Immanuel Kant's

METAPHYSICS

anthropocentric categorical imperative: the human person never should be treated as a means to an end, but the human person should be regarded always as an end in him or herself. This is to say that the human person is the highest good in the order of moral goods because it is the human person who defines moral agency in relation to the Good. A human person should never be used as a means to some allegedly more valuable end of action than that of the person. In such a case, the intended impersonal end would not justify the violation of a human person's dignity by treating him or her as a means (an object) to that impersonal end, whether it be money, progress, or even destroying one human life (no matter how small or compromised) for the sake of prolonging or enhancing the quality of another. Moreover, from a Judeo-Christian perspective, among all of creation, it is the human person who is fashioned in the image and likeness of God—the *imago Dei*—exclusively (see Gen 1:26–27; 5:1; 9:6; Ps 8:6; Wis 2:23; Sir 17:3; Matt 19:4; Mark 10:6; Rom 8:29; 2 Cor 4:4; Col 1:15; 3:10; Jas 3:9).

Along with the sovereign humility of the Good, the personalistic norm escorts moral agents to the fullness of individual and communal flourishing by preventing the reductionism of the person to something less than the person. Utilitarianism, in contrast, is oftentimes content with rendering human persons—especially vulnerable ones—as expendable for the sake of practical goals of utility that promise greater expedience, convenience, and ease for the majority of people in a community. The personalistic norm safeguards against the temptation to interpret fellow human beings as means to lesser ends than the dignity of even one human life. Because practices such as slavery, embryonic stem-cell research, in vitro fertilization, commercial surrogacy, sweat shops, prostitution, human trafficking, pornography, and paying unjust wages use and exploit persons (no

MORALITY

matter how small or vulnerable) as a means to an end, they violate the personalistic norm and break company with the fullness and holism of the Good. The personalistic norm safeguards the rights and dignity of each and every human person, from conception to natural death. Human responsibility grows to the measure that the personalistic norm is operative in moral decision-making and action.

Finally, it is necessary to reference the concepts of freedom, virtue, and vice in relation to the Good. Metaphysics reveals the logical bond between freedom and the Good. The more one does what is good, the freer one becomes. This stands to reason to the degree that the Good generates and preserves the integrity, completeness, and perfection of being. If one does what is good, one heightens the fullness of being. If one does what is evil, one naturally subtracts from this potential fullness of being. Freedom grows in proportion to goodness and the voluntary election of what is good—paradoxical since it is the Good who first calls the moral agent to live in the freedom of the children of God: "It was not you who chose me, but I who chose you and appointed you to go and bear fruit that will remain, so that whatever you ask the Father in my name he may give you" (John 15:16; see Rom 8:21; 1 Pet 2:16). In being elected by the Good and responding affirmatively to this election, one moves from strength to strength (see Ps 84:8). Classical moral theology gives the name virtue (from *vir*, "man, husband, soldier, lover," and *virtus*, "strength, valor, vigor, goodness, bravery, ability, worth, morality, heroism") to this strength. The hero is the virtuous one. The hero binds his or her life to the Good and makes a covenant with the plentitude of being, to live in fidelity to this plentitude and to be at the service of its bounty. The four cardinal virtues are prudence, justice, fortitude, and temperance, while the three theological virtues are faith, hope, and love (see Wis 8:7; 1 Cor 13:13).

If evil is a deprivation of the Good, vice is a corruption of virtue. The seven capital vices (or deadly sins) are pride, lust, anger, greed, envy, gluttony, and laziness. Vice (*vitium*, "fault, flaw, blemish, crime, defect, disorder, sin, offense") is a waning and draining of virtue. It is being compromised and inactivated. It is destructive because it drifts from the fullness of being even in and through its pseudo-activity that is misdirected from the Good and therefore contributes to chaos (disorder) rather than cosmos (order). Vice is the fossil fuel of entropy that, once used up, is irrevocably spent and gone without renewal. As forfeited potency, the only cause that could reactivate being dissipated and distended is pure Act, synonymous with the Good and Being itself, but this reactivation requires a conversion from vice to virtue in concert with the free will of the penitent. The affirmative response to the Good—even as a return to the Good—entails the love of the Good because "all things work for good for those who love God, who are called according to his purpose" (Rom 8:28). Naturally, the Good works for good by way of association and obedience. This is the beginning of a metaphysics of morality wherein the Good is origin and end of all acts worthy of striving.

II. MORAL LAW

Once again, while it is self-evident that the first principle of morality is do good and avoid evil, it is not always self-evident what is good. Discernment is necessary for each and every truly human moral act. Discernment (from *dis-*, "apart," and *cernere*, "to sift") means to sift through possible moral outcomes and determine which alternative is most good. Right reason is necessary for this discernment—reason based on a holistic concept of the Good as informed by metaphysics. Metaphysics involves calling a thing what it is and making ontological distinctions among beings. Metaphysical morality entails applying realist ontology to intentional action. Formal and final causality are integral to this discernment by considering ordered relationships among beings and purposefulness of action according to predetermined ends. Altogether, this is not merely an individual enterprise, but a communal one. Morality is not just a matter of determining for oneself what is good and what is evil. In fact, this concept of absolutely autonomous self-determining morality is at the root of the doctrine of original sin (see Gen 3:1–7). Rather, authentic morality requires a corporate identity in which every individual is part of a greater whole called humanity, and even further, creation.

If morality is not only a "me" thing but a "we" thing, what governs our knowledge of the Good if the Good does not originate with any one of us? In a word, law. Related to terms such as rule, layer, lying down, order, and fate, law encompasses the formal and final causes of morality. Law is what orders just social and ecological relationships by expressing itself through the laws of nature, reason, and divine revelation. Law prescribes ultimate purposes of action and sets due limits on aberrant behaviors that would deviate from the Good and the personalistic norm. Law is paradoxical in how it appears to restrict freedom, but, in the end, promotes the fullness and flourishing of coexisting freedom of individuals in community. After all, saying yes to the Good implies saying no to many miserable and miserly evils. Yet who is the original author of law if not an individual human person? The one who ordained the laws of nature is the same one who predestined the laws of human morality: the Good who is God. Without the working concept of divinity, there is no rational first principle for human morality, other than an arbitrary will to power exercised by those in political power. God, the Good, is necessary for morality, just as God, the *Logos*, is necessary for rationality. What is exhilarating about the intersection of philosophy and theology is that the concept of God is not only a static regulating concept, a postulate of pure reason, or an anthropomorphized ideal of human ingenuity. Instead, in truth, God is dynamic personal goodness who issues moral commands through reason and revelation that flow directly from the divine way of being from eternity: justice, fidelity, solidarity, righteousness, and responsibility for the other.

A. Eternal Law

For metaphysics, God's eternal way of being is called eternal law. This is the premise that there is no binding law without the first principle of law that is called the Good. There is no striving after goodness without the Good itself, identical to Being itself. The purpose of any beneficial law is to orient us toward the Good. But there is no orientation without a light around which to orient its witness. Again, as the psalmist proclaims: "For with you is the fountain of life, and in your light we see light" (Ps 36:10; see Ps 80:4, 8, 20). Just as eternal Act gives rise to celestial luminaries, eternal Law communicates itself through reason and revelation. Eternal law is not a necessarily admissible empty concept but a full and meaningful productive concept. By eternal law is meant the Good unfolding itself toward rational moral creatures according to a host of virtuous attributes of being. If the integrity of being is built upon the Good, then it is necessary for the Good to indicate the ways of being that advance the integrity of being. Eternal law, therefore, is not a hidden esoteric (Gnostic!) law that is presumed to be inaccessible to all to the same degree. To the contrary, eternal law is as plain as the first principle of morality: do good and avoid evil. In the first place, the four cardinal virtues originate with and orient toward the Good: prudence, justice, fortitude, and temperance. These are universally good ways of living that forward and increase the teleological perfection of being. Such virtues stem from a general reverence and respect for being and beings. Eternal law, as the eternal agency of the Good, defined by its immutable constancy, sets the perennial standard of value for all law and legislation.

B. Natural Law

Rooted in the laws of nature, and reason attuned to the intrinsic order of nature, natural law marks the first encounter with eternal law. It is obvious that all physical beings operate according to fixed laws of interaction that determine their peculiar formal, material, and ever-evolving corporeal constitution. These laws are not subject to change, but all that changes is subject to these laws. It is because of the stability of natural laws that there can be an instability of mutable forms of matter. We even might speak of the stable instability of mutable forms of matter insofar as the forms themselves are stable in their distinctiveness and the ends toward which all forms evolve are stable in their definitiveness. The stable instability of the laws of nature provoke a response from rational moral agents. How should I act with respect to these immutable laws that shape and define my being in relation to other diverse beings? Since I am not the author of these laws but their witness, I sense a vocation to responsibility as response to their ordination of me in the peculiarity of my personal being. Reason is ancillary in relation to the primacy of natural law. Natural law is not reason itself, but what precedes and summons reason to become reasonable. Reason is response and not rector; it is witness and not creator. Natural law is eternal law inscribed in created and received nature.

C. Human/Civil Law

Every polis, whether national or local, has its laws. There are prescriptions and consequences of action. There are written and unwritten social norms that govern behavior and lend the force of accountability. Legislative social organization promotes the welfare of citizens and marshals a collective movement toward the common good. To the degree that just laws are enacted and enforced, a polis becomes a *plenus* ("fullness") of social being. Without principle or authority (*arché*) there is disorder (*an-arché*). Without law, there is no polis, no nation-state. Yet the concept of law does not originate with the concept of democracy or any other particular form of social organization. In contrast, any form of social organization derives its impetus from the anterior concept of law that empowers the possibility of social organization through its dependence on law. Because, for instance, there is a universal rational understanding of justice—giving one his or her due—there is the potential to organize ourselves around such universal first principles of law and virtue.

Figure 24

D. Divine Law

The seal and certainty of law is divine law. Divine law perfects and completes natural law, and the term refers to the moral prescriptions that come through divine revelation. Specifically, for Judeo-Christian belief, divine law is communicated through Scripture, Tradition, and, above all, Jesus of Nazareth. Because Jesus is *Logos* (reason/word), he also is *Nomos* (law). Jesus is eternal law in the flesh. Jesus is the divine way of eternal being within the created order of finite being. The consistent and coherent pattern of Jesus's life and teachings disclose the concrete and immanent meaning of the abstract and transcendent concept of eternal law. It stands to reason that if the goodness of the Good self-adheres according to eternal law (as emanation rather than limitation), and if the Good orders creation according to eternal law, then it follows that eternal law would be self-communicated, not only through natural law, but also through divine law that deigned to make known in a personal way through personal media the personal solidarity and communion of the three Persons of the Most Holy Trinity. The eloquence and intellectual and affective persuasion of Christianity, especially in the teaching authority of the Catholic Church, is the consonance between natural law and divine law. Truth does not contradict truth, and instead a complementarity of wisdom obtains between reason and revelation. Though the truths of divine revelation surpass the intellectual capacities of reason alone (and so suggest the necessary media of Scripture and Tradition), they do not contradict but coincide with the most sober, lucid, and responsible rationality. Divine law seals and certifies the uprightness of natural law by purifying it of its imperfections as manifest in a fallen, entropic, and atrophied world.

III. CONSCIENCE

Since it is irrational to claim to be a law unto oneself, rational deliberation and divine revelation are put to consciousness as call and proposal. The mode of conscious life that freely interacts with reason and revelation is called conscience. Conscience (from *con-*, "with," and *scientia*, "knowledge") is the manifestation and proclamation of eternal law, not identical to the self, within the self. An innate orientation to the Good subsists in every human subject, even *in potentia* and oftentimes latent or corrupted by bad moral examples and a lack of proper formation. There is a law received from without and a law received from within, and it is one and the same. The eternal law of the Good is attested through the martyrdom of the external witness to beauty, goodness, and truth, and through the martyrdom of the internal witness to the triune transcendentals. An inner yearning that is self-attested as conscience is validated and confirmed by the exterior witness who joyfully embraces and triumphs through the ordeal of truth. Conscience is witness to goodness redoubled as the Good is called into suspicion by the effigy of its shadow. Only the martyr can attest to the self-vindication of the Good that is evidenced in the scarlet blood exposed without reservation or regret to the light of day.

IV. A MORE EXCELLENT WAY

In making the essential connection between the gravity of conscience and the solemnity of the martyr, we are ready to draw this book to a close. Metaphysics supplies the rational reassurance of the super-rational act of heroic witness. To the degree that virtue is a byproduct of fidelity to the Good, the fullness of law prescribes the pattern of the virtuous life. However, there is virtue and there is heroic

MORALITY

virtue. The former tends to stay within the boundaries of the exigencies of nature and right reason in good metaphysical form, but the latter appears to transgress these as it yearns past concepts, categories, and even the wonder of being (in general and in specie) all the way to encounter with persons and a hermeneutics of gift. Divine revelation exceeds ontology by unveiling the interpersonal reason for being that describes the essence of eternal being: love. The zenith of divine revelation is Jesus as Torah transfigured into flesh. Jesus reveals that the eternal law is love—love as self-donation, sacrifice, and faithful responsibility for the other who faces me. Paul the apostle supplies a timeless (because in reference to the fullness of time) account of love in his first letter to the church in Corinth (chapter 13). He prefaces this litany to love (*agápe*) by calling it "a more excellent way" (1 Cor 12:31b). Every good method admits of its non-self-sameness with the Good itself. Metaphysics is a way (*hodós*) that leads to the Good and is not identical to the Good. Good methods and practitioners of these methods are the first to admit that the method is not one with its goal, though having some share in it. Metaphysics is good, but is not the Good. Our final turn to love is a turn not so much away from metaphysics, but a turn within and beyond the manageable capacities of metaphysics. For love is to be understood not only as the formal and final cause of being, but also as the transcendence of transcendence and, therefore, personal immanence and intimacy. This more excellent way of love—more excellent than all of its methodologies and lexicon of predicates—is actualized to the measure that it is performed. Instead of continuing to talk about the art of performance, let us have one in the forms of prayer and poem.

O LORD God, King of the universe and King of my heart, I humbly approach your throne of grace in this time of need. For us creatures, it is always a time of need because we are needy in relation to you, from whom all good things come. You are source and summit of our being, and apart from you we can do nothing. Because you are, I am. I write I am, I say I am, I am I am because you are I AM. You have loved me into being and will love me into eternal life because you can do no other . . . as if eternal love had a choice to love or not. There is only a choice because there is love in the first place. The final decision (which is today's decision) is between love and its lack. I choose love because you chose me. My choice is no new creation, but only an obedient joyful acceptance of the giftedness of my own being and that of every other being, above all, those who face me in the nakedness and vulnerability of their unique and incommunicable faces, who speak their apparition as the prophetic witness to the mission of responsibility that is my own. With Paul Ricoeur, I say, let being be thought in me because Being thinks of me. Yes, LORD, I have a share in being because you are Being from eternity—not Being alone but Being as the divine We: Father, Son, and Holy Spirit. I adore you, O God, and may your Sacred Heart find its pulse in me, and may your Precious Blood flow through my veins all the way to resurrection.

FIVE WOUNDS

Crown him many crowns
Come thief do not cheat
Chaos inversion
Uncaused cause replete

Throbbing is the heart
That loves to entreat
Noble compunction
Repetition beat

That pleads with sinners
The banquet now keep
Humble vocation
Scandal mercy seat

To love love's beloved
Until all complete
Hidden Cistercian
Discalcéd bare feet

Heartstrings aflutter
Wake graveyards from sleep
I am who I am
You are my lost sheep

V. MORALITY INCOMPLETE

Love, as a more excellent way than metaphysics, brings us to admit that metaphysics alone does not suffice to inspire moral perfection. While it delivers the idea of perfection, and indeed its necessity in relation to the realm of becoming, it is unable to describe the lived experience (*Erlebnis/ le vécu*) of moral perfection. In the end, metaphysics may know a great deal but love very little. For what does metaphysics have to do with love? "If I speak in human and angelic tongues but do not have love, I am a resounding gong or a clashing cymbal. And if I have the gift of prophecy and comprehend all mysteries and all knowledge; if I have all faith so as to move mountains but do not have love, I am nothing" (1 Cor 13:1–2). Even though metaphysics does not speak much of love, perhaps it speaks much of being, first principles, causality, cosmology, and morality because of love. Perhaps love is the hidden and quiet meaning of the uncaused cause, pure act and being itself (*ipsum esse*). Yes, this is certainly the case insofar as "God is love" (1 John 4:8, 16b). There is (*es gibt*) goodness because of love. There is (*es gibt*) being because it is good to be and love loves what is good (Rom 12:9). The ultimate cause of all causes is love because "love is goodness giving itself away" (according to Edith Stein). We hardly can speak of the Good and Being itself without reference to eternal Love. Yet metaphysics has no sufficient grammar or concepts that can describe love as experienced. Fortunately there is another method that comes to the assistance of metaphysics to fill out what is lacking: phenomenology.

We have traveled far with metaphysics; however, it is safe to say that most people do not live according to the secluded exigencies of metaphysics, but by the certainties of the flesh and the persuasiveness of matter. Why does matter

METAPHYSICS

matter? It does because matter stimulates, secures, seduces, and satisfies. Matter is satiated by matter, and as long as our bodies are matter, matter will matter. What metaphysics shows us, and what phenomenology corroborates, is that matter does matter, but only in relation to spirit, namely, the love of God.

> Do not love the world or the things in the world. If any one loves the world, love for the Father is not in him. For all that is in the world, the lust of the flesh and the lust of the eyes and the pride of life, is not of the Father but is of the world. And the world passes away, and the lust of it; but he who does the will of God abides for ever. (1 John 2:15–17)

So metaphysics has given us logical certainty that God is, and to some degree what God is, but it was divine revelation that granted access to the knowledge and assurance of who God is inasmuch as we are known by God. In Jesus of Nazareth, God is revealed above all as love. Since metaphysics is unable to describe the experiential givenness and signification of love, we must turn to phenomenology to do so.

This is the impossible task for metaphysics—made possible to the measure that it is willing to humble itself and let itself be bracketed by phenomenology, at least for a time, until it is summoned at the final countdown to pass judgment on what is, even if what is always has been. For the sake of love and mercy, metaphysics must yield. It must stay a premature judgment to empower the *fiat* of the delinquent creature. "But do not ignore this one fact, beloved, that with the Lord one day is like a thousand years and a thousand years like one day. The Lord does not delay his promise, as some regard 'delay,' but he is patient with you, not wishing that any should perish but that all should come

MORALITY

to repentance" (2 Pet 3:8-9). Metaphysics must give phenomenology time to describe, while the wheat and weeds grow together until the time of harvest, when the grain is ripe and the sickle is wielded (see Matt 13:24-30; Mark 4:26-29). Yes, there are apocalyptic and eschatological implications here, but practical ones as well. If we imagine truth to be a house, metaphysics is the front door, the main entrance. Phenomenology, on the other hand, is the back door, the rear (unexpected and unpredictable) entrance to the same house of truth. In our time, we must let these two methods work together in tandem to lead us to the fullness of truth with reference to both logical necessity and common experience.

Figure 25

Only a handful of philosophers and theologians have insisted on this twining of method over the past century: Edith Stein, Hedwig Conrad-Martius, Erich Przywara, Karl Rahner, Hans Urs von Balthasar, Paul Ricoeur, and Karol Wojtyła, to name a few. Twining is an appropriate term to use to refer to the dialectical proximity of method(s) as twining can imply both separation and joining together. Not a synthesis of meta-phenomenology or phenomeno-metaphysics, but a dialectic between metaphysics and phenomenology. Each method must remain its own, but they are called together to converse and to interact. As iron sharpens iron, so one method sharpens the other (see Prov 27:17). Metaphysical morality results in a half-baked morality. It secures the intellectual veracity of eternal law and universal moral norms, but it lacks the descriptive zeal and zest to inspire common folks to moral perfection. In fact, phenomenology prevents metaphysics from drifting into the uninhabited territory of irrelevance because phenomenology convinces the erotic sensibilities of the flesh to become spiritualized as flesh destined for resurrection. It gives (*es gibt*) because there is (*ipsum esse*); because there is (*es gibt*), it gives (*es gibt*). It will be left to another book, *Phenomenology: A Basic Introduction in the Light of Jesus Christ*, to complete what is missing within an ironic metaphysics-limited, metaphysics-alone perspective. May metaphysics heed an exigency not its own and turn to the source of phenomenology to saturate its static concepts and invest them with renewed life and vigor.

> Then he said to me: Prophesy to the breath,
> prophesy, son of man!
> Say to the breath: Thus says the LORD GOD:
> From the four winds come,
> O breath, and breathe into these slain
> that they may come to life.
> I prophesied as he commanded me,
> and the breath entered them;
> they came to life and stood on their feet, a vast army.
> (Ezek 37:9–10)

<u>**Key chapter concepts:**</u> morality, conation, first principle of practical reason (do good and avoid evil), virtue, vice, eternal law, natural law, human/civil law, divine law, conscience, love, phenomenology

MORALITY

QUESTIONS

1. How is it possible to construct a moral worldview beginning with the metaphysical question of being?
2. What is the first principle for morality and why is this principle significant for all moral decisions?
3. Define the four types of law according to metaphysics and describe how all of these types of law are related to one another.
4. What is the role of conscience in the moral life?
5. Why is morality incomplete within a metaphysical framework alone? What else is needed?

INDEX

accident(s), 22, 25–26, 28, 36, 47–48
actuality, 14, 39, 44, 61–63, 77–78, 99, 106
aesthetic, 102
angels, 16, 18, 21–22, 25, 27, 34, 38, 71, 77, 86, 91, 98–101, 108, 125
animal(s), 25, 27, 73, 76, 91, 98
Anselm of Canterbury, 43–44, 56
Aquinas, Thomas. See Thomas Aquinas.
Aristotle, xiv–xvii, xix, 1, 7, 16–17, 22, 26, 36–37, 58, 60–61, 67, 76–77, 89, 91–92, 100
astronomy, xiii, 98
atom(s), 7, 16, 21, 42, 63–64, 66, 71–76, 91
Augustine of Hippo, 39
Avicenna, xv, 27

Balthasar, Hans Urs von, 127

beauty, xv–xvi, 6, 18, 54, 82, 92, 101–12, 122
becoming, 35, 39, 60–61, 71, 76–77, 84–85, 96, 104–5, 125
body, xv, 10, 20, 26–28, 36, 47–49, 55, 68, 74, 76, 97

Catholic, 27, 48, 121
causality, 14, 18, 37, 57–90, 93, 95, 102, 106, 111, 117, 125
chaos, 37, 94, 106, 108, 116, 124
Christian, v, xv–xviii, 26, 29–31, 34–35, 48, 52, 60, 85, 89, 104, 112, 114, 121
Christology, 29, 36, 52, 56
church, xvi, 21, 30, 32, 36, 48, 53–55, 95–96, 104, 121, 123
conation, 102, 107, 128
Conrad-Martius, Hedwig, 127
conscience, xi, 42, 122, 128–29
consciousness, 83–84, 122

INDEX

contemplation, xv, 2, 5, 7, 31, 36, 41, 81
cosmology, 90–108, 125
cosmos, 6, 15, 94, 103–4, 106, 108, 116

Derrida, Jacques, xix
dialectic (or dialectical), 127
Dionysius the Areopagite, 95–96
Duns Scotus, John, 35, 62, 98

ego, 36, 83–85, 101
Einstein, Albert, 63, 65, 69, 89
element(s), xiii, 7, 16, 59–60, 72–73, 91, 97–98, 100
empathy, 33
energy, xi, xiii, 18, 38, 63–64, 69, 71–78, 82, 89, 97, 100
entelechy, 76, 81, 89, 101
epistemology, 60
eschatology, 102, 108
ethics, 110
evil, 37, 41, 110–18, 128
evolution, xv, 8, 10, 55, 63, 71, 93, 108

fiat, 52, 86–89, 126
freedom, 9, 16, 23, 101, 115, 117

geometry, xiii, xvi–xvii, 37, 45–46
gift, 7, 9, 13, 22, 29, 38, 67, 81, 103, 107, 123–25

glory, v, 11, 20–21, 41, 85, 90, 105, 107
goodness, v, xv–xvi, 6, 18, 39–41, 44, 54, 81–83, 92, 101–25
grace, 34, 81, 87, 105, 110, 123

Heidegger, Martin, 66
hierarchy, 28, 92, 95–96, 108
Holy Spirit, 15–16, 29, 34–35, 54, 87–88, 124
Houselander, Caryll, 6
hylomorphism, xvii, 7, 36

infinite, 2, 7, 11, 13, 16, 18, 33, 98–99, 105
intellect, xiii, 16–18, 23, 38, 40, 42–44, 67, 81, 101, 104, 110, 121, 128
intellectual object, 40, 44
intelligence, 82, 89, 94
intentionality, 12, 95, 105, 110
intuition, 5, 19, 35, 38
ipsum esse, 2–11, 14, 28–29, 32–36, 41, 61–62, 66, 74, 78, 80–81, 105, 112, 125, 128

Jewish, xvii, 29, 32, 34
John Paul II, v, 104

Kant, Immanuel, 113

language, xix, 25, 30, 38, 55, 95, 101
Levinas, Emmanuel, xv

INDEX

Logos, xviii, 3, 12, 30, 34, 38, 50, 52–56, 74, 87–88, 104, 106, 118, 121

Mary of Nazareth, 52, 54, 86–89
mass, xiii, 18, 38, 63–64, 72, 74, 78, 82, 89, 97–98
mathematics, xv, 45
mind, xix, 15, 18, 21, 23, 75, 90, 94, 104, 111
morality, 55, 82, 95, 102–3, 109–29
music, xiii, xv, 54

necessity, 79, 89, 125, 127
Neoplatonic, xvi
Nietzsche, Friedrich, xix, 17, 25
nothing, xiii, 1–2, 5, 13–14, 21, 42–43, 55–56, 60, 67–68, 70, 78–83, 87–88, 91, 97, 99, 103, 105, 107–8, 111–13, 124–25

ontology, 3, 53, 93, 112, 117, 123
organism, 8, 68, 74–76, 93, 97

Parmenides, xi
perception, 11, 23, 61, 66
phenomenology, 22, 77, 83, 125–28
philosophy, xiii, xv–xvi, 1, 11–12, 14, 22, 32, 56, 60, 91, 104, 118
Plant, 27, 73, 91, 97–98
Plato, xv–xvii, 71, 102, 108

polarity, 28, 64, 94
possibility, 3, 6, 10, 14, 31, 35, 38, 45, 50, 60, 71, 77, 79, 89, 120
potentiality, 28, 39, 44, 61–62, 99
prime matter, 10, 86
Przywara, Erich, 127

Rahner, Karl, 127
Ratzinger, Joseph, v
reductionism(s), 17, 24–25, 76, 101, 114
revelation, xvii–xviii, 9, 11–12, 14, 29, 33, 35, 44, 52, 55, 61, 77, 92–93, 103–4, 117–18, 121–23, 126
Ricoeur, Paul, 124, 127

soul(s), xii, 10–11, 17, 20–21, 26–28, 36, 47, 54, 74, 86, 100–102
spacetime, xiii, 64–65, 67, 69
Stein, Edith, xix, 11, 14, 39, 63, 65, 69, 83, 89, 125, 127
suffering, 33, 105
supernatural, xviii, 88

teleology, 74–75, 82, 89
Teresa Benedicta of the Cross, v
Teresa of Avila, 20
theology, xiii, xv–xviii, 11–12, 14, 29, 31, 40, 48, 52, 54, 56, 60, 77, 98, 104, 115, 118

INDEX

Thomas Aquinas, v, xv, xix, 3, 35, 43–44, 58–62, 77–78, 82–84, 89, 91, 105
tradition(s), xvi, 1, 9, 31–32, 35, 55, 85, 104, 121

transcendence, 33–34, 40–41, 101, 123
transcendental(s), 82, 101, 108, 122
Trinity, 14–16, 30, 52, 77, 85, 121

universal, xiv, 4–6, 15–17, 22–23, 26, 30, 36, 45, 47, 55, 76, 92–93, 101, 110, 119–20, 128

value, xii, xvii, 58, 102, 119
vice(s), 31, 110, 115, 116, 128
virtue(s), xv, 5, 29, 47, 54, 99, 110, 115–28
vocation, 58, 76, 85, 119, 124

Wallenfang, John, 58
wisdom, xv, 37, 55, 75, 110, 121
Wojtyła, Karol, 127
work(s), xviii, 8, 18, 61, 90, 96, 116, 127

YHWH, 32–33, 36

www.ingramcontent.com/pod-product-compliance
Lightning Source LLC
Chambersburg PA
CBHW022125160426
43197CB00009B/1156